I See Rude People

One woman's battle to beat some manners into impolite society

AMY ALKON

New York   Chicago   San Francisco   Lisbon   London   Madrid   Mexico City
Milan   New Delhi   San Juan   Seoul   Singapore   Sydney   Toronto

The *McGraw·Hill* Companies

Library of Congress Cataloging-in-Publication Data

Alkon, Amy.
    I see rude people : one woman's battle to beat some manners into impolite
society / Amy Alkon.
        p.   cm.
    ISBN-13: 978-0-07-160021-7
    ISBN-10: 0-07-160021-3
    1. Courtesy.   2. Etiquette.   I. Title.

BJ1533.C9A45   2010
395—dc22   2009023165

3 4 5 6 7 8 9 10 11 12 13 14 15 16 17 18 19 20 21   DOC/DOC   0 9

ISBN-13: 978-0-07-160021-7
ISBN-10:   0-07-160021-3

McGraw-Hill books are available at special quantity discounts to use as premiums and sales
promotions or for use in corporate training programs. To contact a representative, please e-mail
us at bulksales@mcgraw-hill.com.

In memory of Catherine Seipp

CONTENTS

1   **RUDE AWAKENING**   1

2   **LET THE SHUN SHINE IN**   21

3   **IT ALL STARTED WHEN FRED LOPEZ STOLE MY PINK CAR**   37

4   **THE MOBILE SAVAGE**   55

5   **THE BUSINESS OF BEING RUDE, PART 1**   73

6   **THE BUSINESS OF BEING RUDE, PART 2**   103

7   **THE UNDERPARENTED CHILD**   115

8   **IT'S ONLY FREE FOR TELEMARKETERS TO CALL YOU BECAUSE YOU HAVE YET TO INVOICE THEM**   139

9   **MODEMS WITHOUT MANNERS**   165

10   **IT'S NICE TO BE NICE**   193

    ACKNOWLEDGMENTS   211

1

RUDE AWAKENING

Yes, Barry, it's me, a total stranger, calling you on your cell phone.

"Who are you? Who are you?" Barry asked, again and again. "I don't know you."

"No, you don't, but I know lots of things about you, Barry! Yes, I know lots and lots of personal details about you . . . down to your name and phone number, which you shouted into your phone at Starbucks, not caring in the least whether the rest of us wanted to hear all about you or not."

Barry was speechless—for a change.

"Just calling to let you know, Barry, that if you'd like your private life to remain private, you might want to be a little more considerate next time! Bye!"

Just because you have a self doesn't mean you should express it. I know, I know . . . as the Barrys of the world, commandeering the airspace of every coffee shop, grocery store aisle, and post office line inform me, "IT'S A FREE COUNTRY!" "IT'S NONE OF YOUR BUSINESS!" And then, there's my favorite: "IT'S A PUBLIC PLACE!" Yes, Barry, it is, which means you share it with a lot of other people—people who'd rather not have their thoughts bullhorned away by the revelation that you're in Starbucks, you'll be home at six, and you have genital warts.

We're all sick of this, yet it's the rare person who squeaks out a word of protest to the perps. If anything, when I shush a cell phone bellower or ask them to pipe down, some other restaurant or café patron being forced to listen to them will come to their abuser's defense, snapping at me, "If you don't like it, go to the library!" (Uh, I wasn't aware the librarians had started serving breakfast—and besides, the library is no place to escape all the asshats yakking it up on their cells.)

What gives? Did somebody put something in all the latte foam that gave the entire nation Stockholm syndrome, where the hostage goes all cuddly on their kidnapper? It seems so simple to me: We need to tell these thought-snatchers that our attention doesn't belong to them, that their right to have loud, dull cell phone conversations ends where our ears begin.

When I ask the brave defenders of others' noise pollution if they're actually enjoying it, nobody ever stands up, pounds their chest, and says, "I *live* to hear some lady take over the psychiatrist's waiting room with the story of her car trouble!"

Picture a woman, early 50s, voice all broken glass and gravel, shouting into her phone and out to a captive audience of patients,

patients' friends and families, all of them reading magazines and talking in low tones to one another. And lucky you, you only have to picture this. I was one of 15 or so hostages forced to listen to the woman power-babbling into her phone for 20 minutes straight:

> Shut up and listen! Cars have four motor mounts, not five.
> So, I should go over to Eddie's and have him drive the car
> around the block. And I'm at Dr. Jaffe's and maybe I'll come
> over when I'm done. . . . I won't throw a fit! I won't throw a
> fit! . . . Just give me five minutes. Can you do that? Can you
> do that? . . . That's fine . . . that's reasonable. Okay . . .
> alright.

Okay . . . alright . . . so that was one situation where I kept my big red trap shut. Since the woman was waiting to see a shrink, I figured there was a chance she was not only madder than a bag of ferrets, but violent, too. I likewise make it my business to just suck it up whenever somebody barking into a cell phone is wearing one of those gangland shower caps or looks like they might be armed. But, what's weird to me is how many people *always* suffer in silence, even if it's just a 13-year-old mall brat "like, yeah, ya know"-ing so loud in line behind them that it's impossible to hear the counter guy trying to take their lunch order.

If it isn't fear of bodily injury that keeps people from speaking up, it's probably fear of verbal confrontation, or maybe they're just not that practiced at it. I'm a syndicated advice columnist with somewhat controversial views, so I regularly get mail from readers that opens with something like "Dear Bitch." (If you're going to refer to me as

"Bitch," maybe drop the "Dear"?) I guess it's a little easier for me to take the heat after telling somebody, usually in somewhat politer terms, to put a muzzle on it.

Just Call Me Revengerella

Perhaps you're picturing me as a little redheaded girl marching around telling the grownups where to put their teaspoons. It really wasn't that way. In fact, I'm no more educated in that sort of etiquette than the average person, and for most of my life, I didn't pay much attention to rudeness. And then, one day, I can't pinpoint exactly when, I just couldn't take it anymore. Overnight, I was like that "I see dead people" kid, except it was "I see rude people." They were everywhere. And they weren't just on cell phones. Cell phone rudeness is just the most prevalent form of modern mannerlessness, or what I call "the new rudeness"—people wildly indifferent to other people. Like Peter Parker, bitten by a radioactive spider and turned into Spiderman, I was transformed: Amy Alkon, nice Midwestern girl, became Amy Alkon, manners psycho, the illegitimate child of Miss Manners and Johnny "Jackass" Knoxville. And, not long afterward, at a Venice, California, Starbucks, a boor named Barry started taking his calls outside.

Barry's just one tiny link in the great, rude chain of being. There's a meanness, a hostile self-centeredness, that's overtaken our society since around the turn of the millennium, and nobody's safe from all the pushing, shoving, and shouting. Contrast the age-old notion of respect for the elderly with "Outta my way, Gramps!"—the message shoppers at a Los Angeles Trader Joe's supermarket sent as they nearly flattened a frail little old man in a walker in their rush to get to the organic veggies.

Now, maybe you're feeling a wave of smug rising in you, those of you who don't live in New York or Los Angeles, suspecting this new rudeness is just one of those big bad coastal city things. Sorry, but when I travel in America, even when I go back to the Midwest, I experience it: "The land of the free" is now the land of the free to be rude, and what used to be called "common courtesy" is getting to be about as common as suburban sightings of the spotted owl.

Assholes Go Back Farther Than Aristotle

Yeah, yeah, yeah . . . once again, somebody's sounding the alarm that civilization's going down the tubes. So, what else is new? Humans probably developed speech largely so they could tell each other to shut the hell up already. And probably since early humans grunted their first words, somebody's been shrieking that the world's about to end, and more often than not, blaming that perennial menace, The Teenager:

> I see no hope for the future of our people if they are dependent on the frivolous youth of today, for certainly all youth are reckless beyond words . . . exceedingly (disrespectful) and impatient of restraint.
>
> —Hesiod, 700 B.C.[1]

---

1 There's some chance this quote is made-up, like others on delinquency attributed to Socrates and Plato, but it's correct in principle, according to history books on ancient Greece; for example, Sir Kenneth Dover's *Greek Popular Morality in the Time of Plato and Aristotle*. Dover writes about youth in ancient Athens: "The characteristic behavior of young manhood was compounded of extravagance, pugnacity, thoughtlessness, drunkenness and sexual excess."

There's more to recent rudeness than some 21st century version of kids street-racing their chariots through the middle of town, listening to death-lute, and tossing their ouzo bottles into some nobleman's yard. Just like teens throughout time, basically doing their thing without a whole lot of thought for anybody else's thing, today's unruly teenagers are bush-league bad-mannered compared to legions of grannies, grandpas, well-dressed businessmen, suburban mommies, and the 40-something woman who came within inches of crashing her Volvo station wagon into my car while simultaneously trying to park with one hand and yammer into the cell phone she was holding in the other.

When I beeped to keep her from swerving into me, she vigorously and repeatedly flipped me the bird (I guess to punish me for existing, and directly behind her to boot). For her grand finale, she exited her car in workout gear, toting a yoga mat, and snarled back at me, "Just off to find a little inner peace, you redheaded bitch!"

Uh, have a nice day!

Meet Homo Barbarus

I call it the "Verizon made 'em do it! defense"—blaming the recent surge in rudeness on advances in technology like cell phones, the Internet, and mobile sound systems that shake the foundation of your house whenever some jackass in a tricked-out Lincoln Navigator turns his radio on in your zip code.

Technology isn't to blame. It just allows rudeness to be spread farther, faster, and to a wider audience. The unfortunate truth is, rudeness is the human condition. We modern humans are a bunch of grabby, self-involved jerks, same as generations and generations of humans before us. It's just that there are suddenly fewer constraints on our grabby, self-involved jerkhood than ever before.

Few people understand exactly how far we *haven't* come. While it may seem like just yesterday that the phone company's "Reach out and touch someone" morphed into the cell phoner's "Reach out and annoy the crap out of everyone," today's projectile bad manners probably date back about two million years. That's the time period from which anthropologists and archeologists unearthed the first traces of humanity, our near-human redneck cousin, Homo Erectus, and the beginnings of behavior and social structures that are more human than ape—making fire, using tools, cooperating to find dinner, and maybe even speaking: "Hurry and invent the wheel so I can get me a pickup with a gun rack and stop chasing squirrels with a sharpened bone!"

Sure, in a couple years, you'll probably be able to e-mail your vacuum cleaner to ask it to be a dear and get the tuna casserole started, but psychologically we're still back in the cave awaiting the invention of the broom. Evolutionary psychologists Leda Cosmides and John Tooby explain in "Evolutionary Psychology: A Primer" that contemporary humans are working off some seriously obsolete mental software; or, as they put it, "Our modern skulls house a Stone Age mind." By this, they mean our brains are programmed to respond to 21st century problems using the adaptations that best solved prehistoric hunter-gatherer mating and survival issues.

Flash forward to now, and our old-world genes can't quite make sense of all the "evolutionarily novel" stuff in our world. Regular famines have been replaced by all-you-can-eat buffets, and just as we're becoming less and less physically active, our Stone Age brains are barraging us with mental pop-up ads: "Eat, eat! You'll never know when you'll see the next Ho Ho!" Then there's the way the news cycle revolves around important global developments like whether Paris Hilton is wearing underpants. Back when our ancestors were hiking across the Sahara, survival was precarious and dependent on the cooperation of one's tribe members, so humans evolved a mechanism compelling us to be nosy about people we know. Unfortunately, our quaint little Pleistocene brains aren't wired to differentiate between people we know and people we know from movies and TV.

Might our brains *get* wired for 21st century living? It's unlikely; at least, not in the 21st century. There is evidence that human biological evolution did not stop in the Pleistocene era; for example, the discovery of changes in the human genome that occurred within the past 500 to 15,000 years, apparently in response to shifts in the human environment. Peter J. Richerson, a professor of environmental science and co-author of *Not By Genes Alone*, points to the advent of agriculture 10,000 years ago, then the domestication of cattle, and the subsequent evolution of a gene in people in cattle-raising regions giving them the ability to digest lactose, the sugar in milk.

But, modern advances, especially modern medical care, have mucked things up. It used to be just the "fittest"—those best mentally and physically suited for the challenges of their environment—who survived to pass on their genes. Today, you could be born without arms, legs, and a left lung and you still might make it.

Further complicating the issue are the rapid changes in our environment in the past 10,000 years. Evolutionary psychologist Satoshi Kanazawa believes it's been changing too rapidly for evolution to catch up. In *Why Beautiful People Have More Daughters*, he and co-author

Alan S. Miller write that "evolution cannot work against moving targets . . . it requires a stable, unchanging environment for many, many generations." By this, they mean small, isolated populations that stay in the same place, reproduce amongst themselves, and do the same kind of work for generations upon generations. That describe anybody you know? Even if it did, as another evolutionary psychologist, Donald Symons, writes in *The Adapted Mind*, "Natural selection takes hundreds or thousands of generations to fashion any complex adaptation." In other words, don't count on everybody's genes getting the message to upgrade their operating system to Cave 2.0 anytime soon.

The Extremely Selfish Gene

People don't just blame technology for social problems, they idealize living without it. The more high-tech and complex our world gets, the more people tend to romanticize "the simple life." Now, maybe you're a better person if you live in a cabin in the woods with no TV, electricity, or running water—or maybe you're Ted Kaczynski. Kaczynzski, a.k.a. the Unabomber, now lives in more modern surroundings—a federal prison where he's serving a life sentence for maiming and murdering numerous people to sound the alarm about the "tyranny" of a high-tech society.

We have a tendency to get all misty-eyed about early men and women, painting them as "noble savages," living in Bambi-like harmony with nature while selflessly looking out for each other. The reality? They had the same genetically programmed tendencies to lie, sneak, steal, cheat, and behave like thoughtless buttwads that we do today. But, back then, being seen as greedy or narcissistic or being caught scamming another member of your band could get you voted out of the cave and forced to go it alone—very likely a death sentence in an environment not exactly rife with Motel 6s and 7-Elevens.

Back in cave days, they didn't have cops patrolling the hood, and not just because there were no such things as blue uniforms, badges, or even shoes. Life was one big Neighborhood Watch program. Humans lived in small tribes where they traded favors (you scratch my hairy back and I'll scratch yours), and had self-interest and a group interest in rewarding cooperation and policing free-riders.

You can't get away with much in an environment where everybody knows you. In contemporary terms, it's like living in a small town your whole life, then robbing the bank, and having half the customers go home and call your mother. For much of human existence, life with other humans was life in a small town where everybody knew your mother. Unless there was a plague or a famine or the Cossacks were coming, people pretty much stayed put and had families that stayed put. While the railroads and mass production of the automobile allowed for somewhat increased mobility, they didn't move people fast enough over great distances to make it attractive for many to uproot themselves from their familial moorings.[2] So, even in the 20th century, in the United States, many people were born and died in the same house, or on the same street, or just a few miles away.

---

2 Even today, a train from Philadelphia to Los Angeles takes 62 hours and 26 minutes—the better part of three days—for a round-trip coach seat fare of $386, while round-trip flights with one stop via Frontier, Northwest, US Air, United, and other airlines can be had for under $300, and get you across the country in just under seven hours.

This began to change after 1949, the year when Pacific Southwest Airlines, the first successful budget carrier, opened its doors in San Diego. They used a Marine Corps latrine as their reservation center, weighed luggage on a bathroom scale, and charged passengers $15.60 to fly from San Diego to San Francisco. In 1971, in Texas, Rollin King and Herb Kelleher started the low-fare Southwest Airlines, with the goal of making flying between two points less expensive than driving. And then, in 1978, the airlines were deregulated, and in the decades that followed, ticket prices dove and kept diving, and vast distances shrunk fast. For the first time, ordinary people had access to cheap, easy, extremely rapid transit across thousands of miles. Air travel, formerly the province of the few and the rich, became more like flying by Greyhound.[3]

Moving across the continent from your family now means living only a few hours and a few hundred dollars away. Cheap or free long-distance phone service and the Internet help bridge the miles. So, if you're like a lot of us these days, your friends and family are scattered like piñata confetti around the country, the continent, and even the globe. Maybe you know a few of your nearest neighbors, but probably not for long, as the days of working for one company for a lifetime are no more, and your neighbors are likely to move or be transferred.

---

3 Of course, in recent years, air travel has become like flying *below* Greyhound—in the baggage compartment under the bus. There are those who still find coach seats adequately roomy; mainly small-boned children under eight, and armless, legless midgets. Better hope you have one of the latter seated next to you, and not some 300-pound man who wordlessly annexes half of your seat like he's Germany and you're Poland.

If you live in a housing development, you probably get from place to place encased in an automotive bubble. Unless you frequent a bar or coffee shop, you may go an entire day or days without running into anybody you know, and the same goes for many or most of the people you speed past in your car. More and more, we're all living in endlessly sprawling areas that would more accurately be called "strangerhoods" than neighborhoods.

Now, I'm not arguing against affordable airplane travel. In fact, I find it completely thrilling that you can hop a big winged bus in Los Angeles and get off that big winged bus in New York five or six hours later. I've also taken advantage of the bonuses of not living in a small-town world, like being able to reinvent myself and escape my nerdy loser past. But, we have a serious problem on our hands: The societies we live in are too vast and too transient for our poor little Stone Age brains. As much as it seems we're ruder than ever, human nature really hasn't changed; in a matter of decades we've just spread out to the point where our genes tell us common courtesy is optional.

We have to do something, and fast, to counter the way our societal sprawl is out of whack with our mental and psychological limitations for rudeness management. Understanding what these limitations are is the first step. And that starts with a bit of nit-picking.

It Takes A Village
(of no more than 150 people)

Got lice? If you're an ape, having a wee infestation actually isn't a bad thing, as it helps you know who your friends are. Yes, while humans invite each other over for cocktails or to share nachos and a six-pack and watch the big game, our hairier primate relatives bond over bug-picking: "Well, hello . . . what's that wriggling in your fur? Mmmm, tasty!"

The average ape can make a habit of picking nits out of the fur of only so many fellow apes. It seems apes' nit-picking collectives—the number of apes hanging out together on any regular basis—have built-in occupancy limits. Evolutionary psychologist Robin Dunbar looked at studies of apes and other primates and found a link between brain development and the size of the groups they're able to live in. The size of the neocortex, the brain's reasoning and communications center, appears to correspond to the maximum number of fellow critters they can maintain a relationship with without chaos and violence breaking out.

Dunbar predicted that the largest workable group size for humans would be proportionately larger corresponding to humans' proportionately larger neocortex. He did a bit of math (the fancy kind that looks like chickens walked through ink, then did expressive dance on a sheet of paper) and came up with 148.7 humans per group—or, give or take 1.3 people, 150.

This 150-person group size shows up again and again in evidence anthropologists and archeologists were able to piece together from hunter-gatherer societies in the past. Since there isn't exactly a mother lode of hunter-gatherer demographic data from the Stone Age, Dunbar looked at the populations of 21 hunter-gatherer societies still in existence around the world. Right in line with his prediction, he found an average of 148.4 people living in each village. Dunbar points out that this is also about the number of living descendants (plus descendants' spouses) that an ancestral couple would have produced after four generations. But, in *Grooming, Gossip, and the Evolution of Language,* he conceded that "it is one thing to show that these groupings exist in the small-scale societies of hunter-gatherers. It is quite another to suggest that they are characteristic of *all* human societies."

Armed with this 150 figure, Dunbar started poking around in human history to see whether it popped up anywhere else. Did it ever. Dunbar discovered that "most societies have some kind of grouping of about this size," from hunter-gatherer communities, to villages in traditional farming societies, to our world, where, in a small-scale study, researchers found a mean of 154 people on people's Christmas card lists.

Dunbar's 150 shows up in war, in peace, in business, and religion. Most armies, including the Roman army and armies from the 16th century to the present, have a basic unit of about 150 men. Dunbar also points to a "well-established principle in sociology" in which social groupings of more than 150 to 200 people are said to require authority figures of some sort to ensure adherence to the rules. Conversely, Dunbar notes, businesses with fewer than 150 people can be organized informally, and can rely on personal contacts between people to channel information and manage employees.

A company that recognizes this is Gore Industries, maker of Gore-Tex and other high-tech products, cited for the 11th time as one of *Fortune* magazine's 100 best companies to work for in America in 2008. According to a University of Virginia case study,[4] company founder Bill Gore believes there's "a precipitous drop in cooperation"

---

4 Joseph Harder and D. Townsend, W.L. Gore & Associates, pp. 1–9. Available at SSRN: http://ssrn.com/abstract=910771.

at the point a group gets so big that everyone no longer "knows" everyone else (around the 150-person mark), and he limits occupancy in his plants to 200 people.

Finally, the Hutterites, a fundamentalist religious group living and farming communally in states and provinces on the U.S./Canadian border, regard 150 as the maximum size of their communities. "They explicitly state that when the number of individuals is much larger than this, it becomes difficult to control their behaviour by means of peer pressure alone," Dunbar explains. "Rather than create a police force, they prefer to split the community."

As compelling as it is that this number shows up all over the place, and that people who've never heard of Robin Dunbar echo his notion that there's something unmanageable about groups of more than 150 people, Dunbar's research isn't at the point where he can definitively say there's a 150-person social ceiling hardwired into human psychology. Still, it seems pretty clear that Dunbar—and the Gore family and the Hutterites and the rest—are on to something.

Whatever the exact limit of human social relationships might be, you have to admit, you behave differently when nobody's looking. Or, okay, maybe *you* don't, but most people do. And thanks to modern human transience and societal sprawl, most of us spend a good bit of time in situations where lots and lots of people are looking at us, but, in effect, nobody's looking, because we're nobody to them and they're nobody to us.

Meaner Pastures

In 1968, a UC Santa Barbara biology professor named Garrett Hardin wrote an essay about overpopulation called "The Tragedy of the

Commons," inspired by the lectures of an 18th century Oxford econ professor, William Forster Lloyd. Hardin's piece could've been less politely but more descriptively titled "The Tragedy of the Asshole in the Commons." He describes a situation where there's a resource, owned by no one person and shared by many. When somebody takes more than their fair share, all suffer the consequences. Hardin uses Lloyd's example of cattle grazing on communal pasture lands. If one or more herdsmen allow their cows to eat all the grass, it ruins the pasture for everybody, and all the herdsmen's cows keel over and die.

Humans, remember, are genetically programmed to look out for numero uno: "Screw you and your cows. I'll be richer and eat more sirloin if my cows eat all the grass." But, as Robin Dunbar and others have shown, our programming to be self-serving jerks is mitigated when a resource is shared by people in a small and consistent community—not because that changes natural human self-serving jerkishness, but because it forces people to act more communally. Basically, you might need the farmer next door at some point, so you'd better not let your cows scarf all the grass and make his cows starve.

Now that we're no longer living in small and consistent (and thus self-policing) communities, private property can be a solution to The Tragedy of the Commons—for example, buying pastureland and letting your cows graze there as needed. These days, most of us do have private property, owned or rented, and don't have cows. But, there are some resources that remain shared, like the air and the oceans, and the airspace in a café. Yes, the café is owned by somebody, but it's set up to be a space that's enjoyed by many. When one person seizes the airspace there as his own—shouting into a cell phone, having a loud conversation or argument, or allowing his underparented child to see if he can crack plate glass windows with his screams—the shared environment is diminished for all.

In other words, rude people are actually stealing from the rest of us by taking communal resources as their own. That's right—the rude are robbing us daily, usually in broad daylight, and without even bothering to slip on a plastic Richard Nixon mask first. And why wouldn't they? They can count on most of us to just sit there and take it like bewildered sheep.

The problem is, we've never had the need we do now for, well, sky marshals of the café, the grocery store, the bus stop, and the dentist's waiting room. Because the need for such novel behavior—strangers policing strangers—is way beyond the pay grade of our vintage genes, we may as well have been dropped into a state dinner on the planet Xerxes and told to follow the usual protocol. Consequently, most people are not only clueless about what to do about public rudeness, they feel they have no right to tell other adults how to behave (save for life-or-death exceptions like "Don't shoot!").

Complicating matters is the fact that solving a crime starts with understanding that a crime has been committed. The nature of what we're being robbed of makes that difficult. It's all colorless, shapeless, massless stuff we can't see, touch, or own, like time, public space, peace of mind, and a pleasant afternoon (which maybe you were having until you got to the dry cleaner minutes before closing, only to find both of their customer parking spaces straddled by a single diagonally parked Porsche). But, your time is valuable, your attention is valuable, and your peace of mind is especially valuable. Recognizing that they have value means you're more likely to value them in the moment they're being yanked from you and do something about it.

Best of all, if you stand up for yourself against the social bullies, you'll be standing up for the rest of us, too.

I can guess what you're thinking: "Come on, lady, unwad your panties and get on with your day." The thing is, there's more to an episode of rudeness than its effect on the individual or individuals who are victims in the moment. Like those grapefruit-of-the-month clubs, rudeness is one of those "gifts that keeps on giving." Consider the parking-hogging Porsche driver. Protecting his car from dings and dents comes at a price, and he's unilaterally decided to make you pay it. But, the price-paying doesn't stop with you. After you drive around and around, futilely seeking a metered spot, then head home without clean clothes to wear to work the next morning, you probably won't be smiling and whistling all the way. In fact, you're likely to flip the bird or lay on the horn at some absent-minded driver, and maybe yell at your spouse, the kids, or the dog when you get home. But, it doesn't stop there. Maybe a driver you raged at goes on to bark at his assistant, who snaps at the guy in the mailroom, who goes home and yells at his wife, the kids, or the dog. Ugly breeds ugly. And not just on the exterior.

These social bullies may actually be poisoning us. Anger is expressed not only on a visceral level but on a chemical one, with a surge of the fight-or-flight hormone cortisol. Studies suggest that consistently high levels of cortisol can compromise the immune system and even lead to a high risk of heart disease. In other words, yes, these boors could literally annoy you to death.

Rudeness isn't just contagious; it's epidemic. An aggressive lack of consideration for others is spreading across this country like a case of crabs through a sleepaway camp, and there isn't a lot standing in the way. We have plenty of laws to combat serious misbehavior, and signs like "No shirt, no shoes, no service," but in most social situations, there's just an unspoken understanding of the right thing to do. Think about it: Despite the absence of printed directions, when's the last time you saw some guy stride up to the pastry case, unzip, and do his business along the side?

People understand how they're supposed to act because of "social norms"—what's generally understood to be acceptable behavior because it's how everyone, or almost everyone, behaves. But, every time somebody engages in some form of social thuggery, they make it that much more acceptable for somebody else to do it. Others begin to imitate their behavior unthinkingly, or feel stupid or silly for feeling some compunction about following their lead. Consider the boors yammering into cell phones in public places, and never mind anybody else there. Others witness their inconsideration, and even if they were raised to be considerate of those around them, and would've been likely to whisper or take their phone conversation to the sidewalk, there's a psychological push to think, "Oh, that's what people do. I'm not going to be the lone dupe who goes outside to talk."

Perhaps, in light of all this—from the way the communities we live in seem too big to be managed by our brains to the extent to which social norms have already been degraded—our prospects sound pretty hopeless. They're actually not. If we're increasingly finding ourselves residents of Meanland, it's only because we aren't doing anything to change that. We get the society we create; or rather, the society we let happen to us.

2

LET THE SHUN SHINE IN

W hat good is knowing that we're living in societies way too big for our brains if there's really no reasonable way to change that? I mean, what are we going to do, ship 99.999 percent of New York City back to Poland or Cleveland or Potsdam or wherever they or their ancestors came from, then prohibit the people still left from interacting with more than 150 people—ever?

Although we can't physically re-create a society more in tune with our psychological limitations, the good news is, we can artificially re-create it. What we have to do is mimic the psychological effect the small town/small tribe environment has on people behaving badly—how the possibility of being caught, shamed, and losing status or getting booted from the fold dissuades people from getting their rude on. And again, while social exile today isn't the death sentence it would have been back in the Stone Age, our genes are still playing and replaying the same old tune in our heads: "It's hard out there alone on the savannah, dude!"

Ironically, the road back to the civility of the 150-person village goes straight through the Global Village. It takes only the Internet and one pissed-off person with a cell phone camera to strip some willful jerk of the protections of obscurity. The pissed-off person posts the photo on their site or one of the many jerk-exposing sites cropping up, and with a little linkie-love from a few bloggers and maybe a news story or two, the perp gets his (or hers).

That's what I tried to do to Mr. Fancy-Van, the guy in the brandnew Range Rover who was menacing me one evening on my drive home. My lane was moving really slowly, so I moved into his—with plenty of room to do it. I suspect the guy was steamed that I dared slow him down even one tiny car-length, and he sped up inches away from my back bumper and stayed on me like that for about half a mile.

I was scared, of course, and upset, and on a faster-moving road or freeway, I would've pulled over rather than risk ending up hurt or dead. But, it was rush hour on a busy boulevard, and traffic was going only 20 to 30 miles an hour. So, even though I drive a teenyweenie hybrid Honda Insight—essentially a large silver corn niblet on wheels—I decided to stand up to the bully. I bit my lip, stayed in my lane, and kept moving with the speed of traffic. Finally, the Range Rover swerved into the next lane and cut in front of me. And then, I had to laugh.

Now, what's almost as idiotic as driving like a total buttwad with a *1-800-howsmydriving* sticker on the back of your vehicle? Well, that would be driving like a total buttwad with a personalized license plate. When I stopped behind the Range Rover at a red light, I whipped out the little Canon that's always in my purse, and photographed the guy's plate—repeatedly, to make sure I got the shot, and because I wanted him to notice.

The guy's plate.

I'm guessing he did notice, because he took off fast when the light turned, weaving through lanes as much as traffic would allow. Eventually, he stopped at another red light. I rolled up next to him—with plenty of time before the light would change to take a nice clear photo of the guy through his untinted driver's side window. But, before I could pick up my camera, he up and drove through the red light. Yep. From a stopped position. Just cruised right through.

I posted the story and photos of the Range Ruder on my blog in hopes of learning the driver's identity. As I'm writing this paragraph, I still don't know it.[5] But, even if I never find out who he is, my interaction with him isn't without benefit. Just by photographing him, I sent him a message: "People are watching! With 10.0 megapixel Canon cameras!" And by posting the photos on my blog, I sent a message to

---

5 No, of course this particular "The Woz" is not one of my heroes, Steve "Woz" Wozniak, co-founder of Apple Computer. I knew it wasn't Woz, a cuddly computer genius-turned-schoolteacher who never wanted to be "management" at Apple because he couldn't bear to fire people. Nevertheless, I e-mailed his assistant so I could say it wasn't him for sure.

other would-be bullies: that nameless, faceless rudeness might not be so nameless and faceless anymore. If they aren't polite, they'd better at least act polite, or they might end up having their anonymity yanked down around their ankles like a schoolboy's shorts.

"The Woz" runs the red light.

That's the last thing Dan Hoyt was expecting. Hoyt is the serial subway masturbator and raw foods guru *New York* magazine dubbed "Onan The Vegetarian." In August of 2005, a 22-year-old female Web designer, Thao Nguyen, was riding the R train when a guy got on, sat down across from her, and started rubbing his crotch. "He unzipped his fly and grinned," reported *New York*'s Russell Scott Smith. And then he pulled his penis out of his pants.

Nguyen dug into her purse, grabbed her camera phone, and snapped a picture. The guy zipped up and bolted at the next station. Nguyen got off the train and found a policewoman, who took her report but didn't want to see the photo. So, that evening, Nguyen uploaded it to flickr.com and to Laundromatic.net, hoping somebody would be able to identify the guy.

Soon, the Laundromatic page was blanketed with comments from other New Yorkers who'd had similar experiences. More and more sites linked to the post, and within a week, wrote Smith, around 45,000 people had seen the picture. A mere two days after Nguyen posted the photo on flickr, the *New York Daily News* ran it on their front page, and newspapers around the world picked up the story. Other victims came forward, including four women who picked Hoyt out of a lineup. The police charged Hoyt with public lewdness, and he got two years' probation.

Nguyen "spawned a mini-movement of sorts," reported Smith, from a 15-year-old Queens girl who gave her own subway flasher a Kodak moment to a group of male and female Nguyen admirers who started the blog HollabackNYC.com. HollabackNYC, which inspired Hollaback blogs in other cities across the U.S., encourages women to take cell phone photos or videos of street harassers for Hollaback to post online.

I call this "blogslapping" (think bitchslapping via URL—Web-based perp-catching and punishment, all rolled into one). It's a recent phenomenon, the power of the Average Joe to expose wrongdoing and affect change with relatively inexpensive and widely available consumer electronics—like a video camera that anyone with a few hundred dollars can pick up at the corner electronics store.

Some might say the earliest example of this is Abraham Zapruder's 8-millimeter home movie of the Kennedy assassination, but Zapruder caught the shooting by accident while filming the parade. The first major *intentional* example of Average Joe electronic journalism was in 1991, although it wasn't Web-based since only a smattering of uber-geeks were puttering around on what would become the World Wide Web. Los Angeles resident George Holliday, then a manager at a big plumbing and rooting company, was awakened in the middle of the night by sirens. He ran to his apartment window and looked out on four white LAPD officers engaged in the beating of an arrest-resisting black man, Rodney King (who'd just led the officers on a car chase, and who subsequently charged at one of the officers). Holliday turned on his Sony Handycam and rolled the videotape—the videotape that was aired, seen, written, and talked about around the world.

The broadcasting of the tape led to the trial and eventual acquittal of the officers—in Simi Valley, a conservative, white-on-white bedroom community of Los Angeles. Blacks were enraged by the verdict, suspecting from the start that Simi Valley was no place for a fair trial, and the racially driven L.A. riots flared—six days of looting, arson, robbery, and murder.

The four officers were later retried on federal civil rights violations, and two were convicted. Officer Laurence Powell, who brutally clubbed King with his baton numerous times—including in the face, aga nst LAPD policy, and typed on his patrol car computer, "I havent [sic] beaten anyone this bad in a long time"—was found guilty. Sergeant Stacey Koon was the supervising officer on the scene. Koon, a cop with over 90 commendations[6] who'd once given mouth-to-mouth resuscitation to a black transvestite with open mouth sores,[7] and who never beat King and unsuccessfully tried to subdue him by twice tasing him, was also found guilty. All four officers are now off the force.

Ultimately, Rodney King received a $3.8 million court settlement from the City of Los Angeles. *The New York Times* reported that a direct mail campaign for Stacey Koon raised more than $1 million,

---

6 Madison Gray, "The L.A. Riots: 15 Years After Rodney King: Stacy Koon," *Time* (April 25, 2007).

7 Lou Cannon, *Official Negligence: How Rodney King and the Riots Changed Los Angeles and the L.A.PD* (Boulder, CO: Westview Press, 1999).

and possibly as much as $4.7 million, to pay his legal bills and support his wife and children while he was in prison. Holliday, on the other hand, told the *Los Angeles Times'* Michael Goldstein that he'd earned "a few thousand dollars" licensing his footage to Spike Lee and other film-makers, received plaques from the LAPD and the L.A. County Board of Supervisors, and became a Trivial Pursuit question, with his name misspelled "Halliday." Meanwhile, he got death threats in the mail and kept hearing "You're the guy who caused the riots" from strangers who recognized him in public. His first wife left him. "There was a sea of reporters every day," he told Goldstein. "Maria didn't even want to leave the house." His second marriage also failed.

It's unclear as to which of Holliday's problems trace back to his decision to make the video public. Goldstein reported that Holliday "didn't spread the blame around," but does feel he was abused by CNN and other media, which gave him little credit and no compensation. Holliday also told Goldstein that, as the grandson of a London bobby, he felt uncomfortable about the impact his footage had on the image of the LAPD: "I filmed this tape that makes the police look bad." But then, he added, " . . . Every time a policeman has recognized me, they tell me I did the right thing."

Sergeant You

So, here we have two people—George Holliday and me—who take action when we can't benefit personally and might wind up dead or at least get a broken arm or a bloody nose for our trouble. Clearly, we're both screwy in the head, and maybe even a step or two away from running naked through the library and microwaving the neighbor's cat.

Actually, we're both what economics eggheads call a "costly punisher"—a person who takes it upon himself to go after wrong-doers, even if it's costly for him to do so, and even if he can't expect any personal gain from it. Economists Ernst Fehr and Simon Gächter explain our apparently irrational behavior with evidence from their experiments suggesting that "not all people are driven by pure self-interest." In fact, there seems to be a natural human propensity in some people to punish wrongdoers. Costly punishers are likely to be "cooperators"—people prone to look out for the welfare of other individuals and for the good of the group. We CPs, more than the average person, get enraged when some jerk tries to cheat the rest of us, and our anger motivates us into this do-it-yourself justice, never mind the personal cost.

To test the propensity to punish and how the possibility of being punished affects behavior, Fehr and Gächter set up a classic economics experiment called a "public goods game," which four players would play 10 times, getting an allotment of 20 tokens each time. (Each token represents about five cents in U.S. funds, and all tokens in a player's possession at the end of the experiment are to be converted to real money and paid to the player.)

Each player decides, without informing the other three, how many of his tokens he'll put into a shared "pot." At the end of each game, players keep the tokens they didn't put in, plus their share of the pot, divided evenly among the four in their group. But, tokens have varying values. Once a token is contributed to the pot, it increases in worth by 40 percent, increasing the take-home pay of all the players. So, the more "cooperative" and group-minded they *all* are, the more they all take away in the end.

A "free rider," a player who greedily withholds his tokens, putting little or nothing in the pot, finishes with the most tokens. He not only keeps his initial share but gets a cut of the contributions by the others, coming out on top while diminishing others' take. And, in the version of the game without repeat interactions with the same players—much like many daily interactions in our society, where we're surrounded by strangers—he'll get away with it.

In later games, Fehr and Gächter added the possibility of punishment, informing individual group members how much their co-players had contributed in previous games, and allowed them to mete out punishment on those who were free riders—for a fee. For each punishment point tacked on to a free rider's tally (reducing the free rider's final payout by 10 percent), the punisher's own final payout was reduced by 10 percent. And yet, players punished away, digging into their own earnings to cut down on the take of the free-riding creeps.

It turns out *the mere possibility of punishment* had a substantial effect on the behavior of the players. When there was none, Fehr and Gächter discovered that "complete free riding is a dominant strategy." But, when the opportunity for costly punishment enters the equation, cooperation increases, meaning players are much less likely to selfishly hoard tokens. In fact, Fehr and Gächter found, when players know punishment is possible, "almost complete cooperation can be achieved and maintained although, under the standard assumptions of rationality and selfishness, there should be no cooperation at all."

The benefit from what costly punishers do is a communal one, a "public good." Fehr and Gächter explain public-good–oriented behavior with the example of people standing in a "well-ordered" line.

All benefit from a nice, orderly line where everyone politely waits their turn, but each person has an individual incentive to take cuts.

When punishments aren't likely, you're better off reducing your waiting time by elbowing your way to the front. The same is true if the line falls apart and everybody's trying to elbow their way forward. (If you don't also put your best elbow forward, you'll have a wait far beyond the average waiting time.) Of course, if everybody's trying to get served before their turn, chaos will ensue, increasing the waiting time for all. Plus, being part of a big shovey mass of angry people makes everybody worse off relative to when everybody stands politely, waiting their turn. Of course, this is true both on the group level and on a personal, emotional level. In the words of Lily Tomlin, "The trouble with the rat race is that even if you win, you're still a rat."

If You Can't Be A Costly Punisher, Maybe You Could Be A Slightly Overpriced Punisher?

Very few people have it in them to go Revengerella on the rude the way I do. I completely understand. It's one thing, when playing a game in some economist's lab, to end up short a few points you've put toward punishing token hogs. It's another thing entirely to go after the rudesters in real life. But, in order to have any hope of "putting the civil back in civilization," everybody needs to do their part. If you can't meet me out there on the limb, maybe you could at least volunteer to rake some leaves?

If, on the other hand, you aren't too timid to go after rudesters, but you don't have the time or wherewithal for blogslapping and other stunts, you might just open your mouth and call somebody on their brutishness. My itsy-bitsy strawberry-blonde friend Jill Stewart did that while waiting in line at the drugstore pharmacy. A tall, barrel-chested man with huge muscles started going off on the pharmacist, a skinny, bespectacled little Asian guy. The big guy loomed over the little guy, furious at being kept on hold for 10 minutes when he'd called the pharmacy:

Big Guy: Who do you think you are? Fucking kept me waiting and inconvenienced me and then you think you got the balls to invite me on down here? Sure I came on down! You people inconvenienced me and you are rude and I am the customer.

Little Pharmacist: Sir, if you want me to get the manager I will, otherwise you can stop complaining. We're a busy pharmacy and your wait on the phone was not unusual and you were the one who was rude.

Big Guy: You want me to come over the counter and let you know how I feel?

Little Pharmacist: I don't care what you do, but you're not going to get served any faster.

Big Guy: You disrespected me! You were rude! The fuck you think you are? Fucking place! I'm a busy person and you are supposed to be serving me as the customer! Fucking people! Fucking inconvenienced me!

Burly men in line behind the guy stood silent—perhaps because there's a real risk of getting clocked by some rudester if you're a man. Jill marched her tiny freckled self over to the guy. "Excuse me, Sir . . . I am waiting for my prescription here, and I'd appreciate it if you could tone it down. Nobody needs to hear another customer flinging around the F-word and making his bad day into our bad day. It's really rude."

"But they made me wait 10 minutes on the phone!" the big guy said. "Then that little bitty guy over there was rude, couldn't answer my questions and started saying stuff to me!"

Jill said, "Nothing bad has happened to you, Sir."

"What?" he said.

"You're not actually having a bad time," Jill said. "You're having a normal, everyday kind of day. Everyone here has waited on the phone forever for the pharmacy guy. Do we start threatening people? Do we jump in our car to drive down because somebody is a jerk? No. But you did. And now you are shouting the F-word and threatening to jump over counters. I don't need to listen to that at the end of a busy day, and neither do any of the other people here."

Nobody else said a word. The guy stepped away a few feet, not sure whether the audience was on Jill's side, but realizing it probably wasn't on his. Moments later, the manager showed up and escorted the guy from the pharmacy area.

As for those of you who aren't comfortable going head-to-head with someone, or who don't feel street-smart enough to suss out whether you'll get beaten up or shot in the process, you could offer us costly punishers a little backup. Whatever you can spare. When somebody's shouting into their phone in a restaurant, or when "parents" let their little savages lay siege to an airline cabin, if you can't quite find your way to squeaking "Actually, it's really bothering me, too!" could you manage a "Shhhh!"? At least give the perp or perps a dirty look to tell them whatever they're doing is very uncool—even before one of us manners avengers leaps out of the closet in our shiny lycra superhero suit, or just in case we can't (like, if the lock gets stuck). To be honest, there are times we don't quite have it in us to go for it. If you shake your head disapprovingly, and maybe somebody else does, too, with the force of your collective disgust you just might help us gin up the stuff to tell some boor bothering all of us to knock it off.

But, let's say even a glare or a "Shhh" or a head shake at the offender is a bit much for you. If you can't beat 'em, at least go out of your way to avoid joining 'em, and maybe even lead by example. Take my neighbor. She gets angry at all the little human injustices just like the rest of us. The difference is, she makes a point of refusing to respond to rudeness in kind; essentially, she refuses to let some boorish stranger define who she is as a person. Instead of lashing back, she takes a deep breath and looks to do exactly the opposite of what was done to her. If, say, some driver cuts her off, she'll go out of her way to let somebody else or a few somebody elses in—people who, in turn, probably become more predisposed to let other people in. Yes, instead of an eye for an eye, it's a bunch of smiley balloons for an eye. Pass it on.

But, let's say you're the rude one—screaming with laughter with a couple friends in an otherwise serene restaurant, not because you're typically inconsiderate, but because you got socially sloppy in the heat of the moment. Say somebody at the next table asks you to pipe down. Your first impulse, especially if they didn't put it quite so diplomatically, is probably to tell them where they can put that pipe. Recognize that impulse and plan ahead—plan to sit back for a moment or two and ask yourself whether maybe, possibly, they might have a point.

Of course, even better than conflict resolution is preempting conflict altogether by making a point of treating people—especially strangers—like they matter.

Yes, I'm aware that you have mascara, liquid eyeliner, and five shades of gray eye shadow to apply. But, see that guy in the Ford Focus behind you? He needs to turn left, too. And maybe he'll get to, if you take care to pull all the way up into the intersection like you would if he were your boss or your dad. And about that pile of food and trash you're about to leave on the table at the coffeehouse . . . would you do that if your best friend and her date were about to sit down? ("Hey, have fun with my garbage!") And, put yourself in the place of the flight attendant—when you're lining up for the bathroom by her jump seat, think about how you'd feel with some passenger's butt right in your face. (The saying is "*do* unto others," not "*doo* unto others.")

Miss (Bad) Manners

I am not writing this book from on high, as some shiny emissary of politeness. I do not have perfect manners. In fact, I have rather imperfect manners. I'm a swearer, a honker, and my hand has, on occasion, detached itself from the steering wheel and gestured to other drivers in a less-than-genteel way.

I'm hotheaded, and I have been known to scream at telemarketers and/or to ask them if they have a suspicious vaginal odor—even if they happen to be men. I now make an effort to be civil to the callers—a number of whom are disabled and without a lot of other job opportunities—and pick on the owners of the telemarketing companies instead.

There are other less obvious episodes of Amy inconsideration, like how, when I first got to L.A. from New York, I bought a "classic" car that, on a single ride across town, probably put out pollution to rival the Union Carbide plant in Bhopal. It wasn't exactly the world's most reliable transportation, so I didn't go many places. But, when I did leave the fresh air of Santa Monica for Hollywood, I noticed that my eyes would start burning from the smog, a lot of which I guessed came from all the cars. Whoops.

Since then, I've become much more aware of my surroundings. My reminder to myself goes something like this: Unless you came in for a lunar landing, and stepped out of the NASA module into a crater instead of out of your car and onto somebody's gum, chances are, you are not on the moon. Chances are, you are on earth, a place filled with loads and loads of other people. If you treat them like they matter, maybe they'll be inspired to treat you and other people like you matter, and maybe, just maybe, life won't feel quite so much like one long wrestling smackdown.

A POTTYMOUTH CALLS
FOR BETTER MANNERS

I love language—the seven dirty words, and about seven bazillion cleaner ones. There are those of you who will wonder, how can I write a book on manners if I run around saying "fuck"? The answer is, I don't consider rude language automatically rude. There are times, of course, when it's inappropriate. In fact, there are times when a lot of words are inappropriate, like the word D-I-E-D when my neighbor's four-year-old is in the room.

Some will grab on to the use of "bad language"—even the mildest bad language—as an excuse to dismiss you. When my cable was on the fritz, I had a series of frustrating "customer service" calls (there was little service involved in any of them), and finally said something like "I don't understand why they don't just maintain the damn cable!" The woman on the other end snipped, "Ma'am, if you're going to use that language with me, I'll have to hang up the phone."

The truth is, swear words command people's attention more than other words, and evoke more emotion.[1] And sometimes, as Supreme Court Justice John Marshall Harlan wrote in the "Fuck The Draft" case,[2] "one man's vulgarity is another's lyric" statement, and sometimes the wrong words—the improper and off-limits words—are exactly the right words to convey a particular message. Fuckin' A!

---

1 Steven Pinker, *The Stuff of Thought: Language as a Window into Human Nature* (New York: Viking, 2007).

2 *Cohen v. California*, 1971, appealing the arrest and conviction of a guy who wore a jacket emblazoned "Fuck the Draft" into a California courthouse. The Supreme Court overturned the conviction.

3

IT ALL STARTED WHEN FRED LOPEZ[8] STOLE MY PINK CAR

I haven't always been this one-woman manners SWAT squad. I used to be just a girl, a girl with a very cute set of wheels. But, I came to realize that at the heart of de-ruding our lives is refusing to be a victim. And, for me, that happened the day I walked out of my house and found only a puddle of oil in the spot where I'd parked my pink car.

Unless you're a down-and-out drag queen with a talent for hot-wiring, your first choice of car to steal probably wouldn't be my powder-pink 1960 Nash Rambler, with its white top, a big pink-and-white covered tire on its trunk, and enough chrome to solar-power Encino for several days. Any relatively recent Japan-mobile would chop up into much more cash. If you're just an exhibitionist, why not hijack an elephant and ride it down Wilshire Boulevard at rush hour, with the Pasadena Marching Band and a bunch of majorettes on Dex-

---

8 Not his real name. The Los Angeles Times changed it when they ran my Rambler story in their Magazine in 1999. I could've changed it back, but I'm hoping my thief has gotten his life together, so I'm keeping him anonymous.

atrim? (I can't imagine a judge imposing a long prison term for grand theft elephant.)

My pink 1960 Nash Rambler.

Nevertheless, on the day I was having 45 people over for a party, I stumbled from my house to get a coffee and into one of those surreal moments when the sound drops out and the world grinds to a halt: My Rambler was gone.

I waited a week for it to turn up abandoned. When it didn't, my insurance company gave me temporary use of a rental Taurus. I was embarrassed to be seen driving a car with all the personality of bar code, but I secretly reveled in its modern mechanical charms, especially its automatic windshield wipers, which gave me a near-sexual thrill. (My Rambler's wipers were vacuum-driven and powered by the engine, which meant that you could either see out the windows during a rainstorm or go forward; take your pick.)

I'd bought my Rambler soon after arriving from New York, before I understood the beauty of getting from point A to point B without dropping an axle. I learned fast. But, losing a vehicle has a lot in common with needing to break up with a problem boyfriend; one is inclined to develop convenient amnesia. A close friend and frequent ride-provider helpfully reminded me of the time my car stopped turning left and I had to go from my house in Venice to Sunset Boulevard and Kings Road, and needed directions with only right turns the whole way. Still, I missed my temperamental pink thing.

Late one Sunday evening, a week and a half after my car disappeared, I was buzzing home in my temporary Taurus when I spotted a Rambler station wagon getting a "jump" from a tow truck just two blocks from my house. Rambler people are essentially culties, but in place of toxic Kool-Aid or matching tinfoil hats, we're bound together by our devotion to these quirky cars. If this guy in the stalled Rambler had seen my Rambler he'd remember it. I screeched to a double-parked halt and ran on over.

He was a twentysomething hipster with a face out of those black velvet paintings of big-eyed puppy dogs and a pompadour like John Travolta's in *Grease*. He told me his name was Fred; he was a mural painter, and he was crazy for Ramblers. He said he hadn't seen my stolen car, but he'd be on the lookout. He suggested I call Michael Kozicki, president of Scramblers, the Southern California Rambler club, and Bob Pendleton, another Scrambler, to see if they had any leads.

As I turned to leave, Fred mentioned that he had a line on an "almost cherry" '60 Nash Metropolitan in South Gate for $1,000. A Metropolitan is what my car would look like if I left it out in the rain and it shrank to about a third of its size. I begged him for the owners' number. Fred said he didn't have it; he just knew where they lived. He offered to take me there on the weekend. He took my number and said he'd call on Friday. I wrote down his number and repeated it back to him twice. I was so excited, I nearly tap-danced home.

I couldn't wait until the weekend to call Fred. In fact, waiting 12 hours was too much for me. I called him at 9:01 the next morning. An old man answered and said that no Fred was to be found at his number. I called back a couple more times, praying I'd just dialed wrong. The man politely but sternly repeated that his home is, and always has been, Fred-free.

I was heartbroken. Fred was just another L.A. flake. I taped his wrong number on my wall and willed him to call. He didn't. But the following Wednesday afternoon, my pal Nina did. She was out of breath. "I just saw your car going south on Orange off Beverly!"

I hung up and dialed 911. "My stolen car, license number 3SXY412, is going south on Orange off Beverly!" The 911 operator did not share my enthusiasm. "If officers run the plate, they'll pull it over."

"You don't understand," I protested. "It's going south on Orange right now! This isn't some gray Nissan! It's a powder-pink Rambler! Like a birthday cake on whitewalls! . . ."

"If the officers run the plate . . ."

"Never mind!" I shouted. I slammed the receiver down and stomped around the room. "If you want something done, do it your goddamn self!" I ran for the Taurus. I weaved through traffic on the freeway and zoomed over to Orange, slowing charitably to avoid pedestrians. I drove around for hours, warning dazed dog-walkers to keep an eye out for stolen cotton candy on wheels. My search fruitless, I decided to head home, but first dropped in at the Hollywood police station.

Being a girl, I find in-person visits in such situations to be quite helpful. ("Hi, I have big breasts, will you help me find my car?") The first officer I spoke with, Clint Dona, who happened to own a 1960 Rambler, was especially sympathetic. He and the officers behind the desk promised to tell the beat cops to watch for my Rambler. I felt re-energized, empowered; I was Nancy Drew (as played by Pamela Anderson)!

I waved a flirty goodbye, got back in the Taurus, and meandered through Hollywood side streets toward the freeway. The Melrose Auto Center, a tiny, iron-gated classic car dealership at Melrose and Sycamore, caught my eye. Still in sleuth mode, I mused, "Maybe they pass hot cars." I ran in to take a look. My car wasn't there. Wearily, I turned to leave. A man called to me. "What kind of car do you want to buy?"

"Actually," I said, "I'm not looking to buy a car. My beautiful pink car was stolen, and I'm out looking for it."

"Don't tell me," he said. "Pink Rambler, white top, continental kit?" (That's the covered tire thingy on the back.)

My jaw dropped. "How did you know?"

"A guy tried to sell it to me this afternoon," he said. "And he left his name and phone number."

The car lot man told me that the guy trying to unload my car had called himself Fred Lopez. He copied down the guy's phone number. It was one digit off the number broken-down-Rambler Fred had given me! He described Rambler Fred down to the ducktail. Stunned, I thanked him and sped back to the police station.

I gave Officer Dona the number Fred had given the car lot guy and he looked it up in a special reverse directory. It wasn't listed. Dona told me not to despair and said that Pacific Division, the Venice police, would handle my case.

The next morning, I called Pacific Division and discovered that they hadn't assigned a detective. I clamored for a little attention from auto theft coordinator Michael Fesperman. He assigned not one, but two auto theft detectives; an embarrassment of riches, I thought—until they neglected to return so many calls that I speculated they'd entered the Witness Protection Program.

I decided to shop around for the best police attention I could find. I typed up and faxed all the information I had to Officer Dona, the two auto theft detectives, and a few nearby police stations. Dona said he never got my fax, but I got a call from his colleague, Special Problems Officer Dan McGehee, who said he was eager to work on my case. I promised to keep him up to date on my detective efforts.

A few hours earlier, I'd spoken with Scramblers president Kozicki, who thought Fred might be a young Rambler nut with whom he'd traded car parts. He strained to recall bits and pieces about him—like that Fred had lived with a young woman in a crummy apartment somewhere near USC; that the 10 Freeway was visible from his place. Kozicki had about eight phone numbers for Fred; none was current.

I tried Bob Pendleton, the other Scramblers guy Fred had mentioned. He passed me on to "Ramblin' Johnny" Koppelman, who thought the guy I described might be the one that Phil Rose, yet another Rambler nut, had nicknamed "Kid Fred." Phil couldn't believe that "Kid Fred" would steal a car—until I said the magic words: "mural painter." "That's him!" Phil confirmed.

Phil recalled that Fred had a girlfriend named Alice,[9] who'd attended a certain snooty L.A. prep school, and that he lived around USC. I pored over a map. Was the street Vermont? Normandie? Hoover? He couldn't narrow it down, but he thought all three sounded

---

9 Not her real name, either.

familiar. That was all the lead I needed. I hopped in the Taurus and zipped down the freeway on the first of many pilgrimages, blithely motoring around an area I later learned was the bloody South-Central of gangsta rap and movies.

Residents squinted at me funny as I cruised and re-cruised their neighborhoods, but nobody looked all that concerned, probably because a shiny rental Taurus isn't the car of choice of most drive-by shooters. I told anyone who would listen about my stolen Rambler: mailmen, Sparklett's delivery people, construction workers, cops on patrol, an elderly Russian lady with enormous pink rollers. Nobody had seen my car. After several hours, I slunk home. I was slaving over a hot computer on my advice column when the phone rang. It was Detective McGehee. "We just picked up your car!"

I screamed so loud I hurt my own ears. After I composed myself, McGehee described the Rambler they'd pulled over: continental kit, white top. Then he got into the chrome. By his account, there was a silver hood ornament on this car that was the equivalent of a Frederic Remington bucking bronc sculpture. Much as I wanted to, I couldn't recall anything like that on mine. My stomach churning, I told McGehee a few of my car's quirks—the big plastic horn button under the steering column; the molding on the left side that I'd secured with a paper clip. None checked out. I glumly admitted that it didn't sound like my car.

McGehee described the driver: black pompadour, sideburns. It might be Fred. "How fast can you get here?" asked McGehee. I whipped down the freeway, accompanied by "The Very Best of Aretha Franklin," my favorite speeding music. I finally rolled up on a small crowd of men and women in blue hovering outside a parking garage.

I peeked at the Rambler. It was candy-apple red—freshly painted sometime in the late '60s. (What's a girl gotta do, supply the cops with paint swatches from Home Depot?) The driver looked like he was no stranger to maximum security, but he wasn't my thief.

After that, McGehee became less responsive. I took my frustration out on Fesperman, complaining his detectives wouldn't call me back either. Fesperman responded by assigning my case to "Officer Number 5," a handsome young policeman with huge muscles who was studying to be a detective.

Unfortunately, although Officer Number 5 seemed sincere in trying to help me, it appeared that Pacific Division hadn't saved up quite enough cereal box tops to put him through detective school. Every time he talked to the Rambler boys, they'd complain to me that he seemed "confused," or they'd say something more specific and less kind. Still, he was all I had. I told him my story, faxed him the details, and headed back to South-Central.

That evening I got a real break. Phil Rose had searched his garage and found a note from Fred with a phone number that varied by only one digit from the numbers Fred had given the car lot guy and me. I asked Officer Number 5 to look it up in the reverse directory. "The number you gave me is a 213 number," he protested. "We don't have the Hollywood directory. I'm just going to call him."

"And say what?" I raged. "Hi, Mr. Car Thief, I'm a police officer, would you mind returning Miss Alkon's car?" (because she's a real pain in the ass to all of us at Pacific Division). I begged him to erase the number and forget he'd ever heard of my Rambler.

I called Fesperman to complain. It turned out that the number was unlisted. Fesperman said he'd request a search warrant to get the phone company to hand over the address, a process he said would take 10 days to two weeks. A week and a half later, Officer Number 5 called. He was just starting to fill out the paperwork for the search warrant.

Days passed. I called Officer Number 5 but ended up speaking with one of the elusive auto theft detectives, who informed me that the judge had rejected the search warrant request "because it had a typo." I bit my lip to keep from screaming into the phone that the police couldn't find a mail truck at the post office.

Early on a Sunday evening, a neighbor rang my doorbell. En route to the freeway from USC, he had spotted my car. He had chased and lost it, but he'd gotten the number on the license plate propped up in the back window—OXG624. It was an old black California plate, probably picked out of a junkyard.

I faxed this information to Fesperman and to the Southwest Division, where my neighbor spotted the car. An auto theft detective at Southwest agreed to put out a crime alert to cops in his area—with Pacific Division authorization. I contacted Fesperman, who agreed to issue it and did, two days later.

The following Sunday, Phil Rose called, all excited. Late that afternoon, Fred had left a message about Rambler parts on Phil's answering machine. On a hunch, Phil called Fred back at the number he'd found in his garage. He got Fred's machine, began talking, and Fred picked up the phone! I couldn't believe my good fortune. I immediately rang up Pacific Division: "I just got a tip that my car thief is home." By then, Officer Number 5 had finally tracked down the address. I asked if the Pacific Division boys would get it from him and send someone over to arrest the thief and pick up my Rambler.

"None of the detectives are here right now," the desk person said. "Can you please call back tomorrow?"

"Even Denny's is open 24 hours!" I howled, slamming down the phone.

Frustrated, furious, I was at wit's end. Then it came to me. I grabbed the phone and punched in a number I now knew by heart.

"Hello?" muttered the guy on the other end.

"You stole my pink car," I shouted. "I want my car back! I want my car back now! I know everything about you but your blood type. I even know where Alice went to high school! The only reason I don't have my car right now, and you in jail, is that the police are really stupid. But I'm through with the police. I just called my FBI friend Tom Nicoletti (I really hadn't[10]). He chases terrorists around the globe and makes them wish they'd gone into flower-arranging. He's so pissed off that he has to do something so lame as going after my silly-ass pink car that he'll throw you in jail for grand theft auto for the next 20 years when he catches you. And he will catch you."

I gasped for breath, guppy-style.

Fred seized the moment. "Where would you like your car?" he squeaked.

"On the street in front of my house," I snarled.

It was there in an hour, in horrible condition. Moldings were missing. Every lock was broken. A door handle had been severed. The formerly pristine rose-beige velvet upholstery was splattered

---

10 And he wasn't really my friend, just a nice guy my former Tribeca dry cleaner once set me up with. His name just came to me when I was on the phone with Fred.

with grease spots and wax drippings. Worse, there were white latex paint droplets all over my hood and chrome. I called Fred back and screamed at him. He pleaded that he had only stolen my car because he'd lost his job and run out of money. This really steamed me.

"Don't talk to me about having no money," I bellowed. "I was once so poor that I worked as a chicken!" (I handed out fliers to hostile New Yorkers, if you'll forgive the redundancy.) Fred apologized for what he'd done and offered to give me his Nash Metropolitan. I declined. I didn't want his car, which was probably stolen anyway. I just wanted my car back in its original condition. He promised to trade some favors to have my car repainted.

The next day, a bill for $164 arrived from Rhonda at Premiere Party Rents for the rental tables that were in the trunk when my Rambler was stolen. I rang Fred. "You're costing me a lot of money. You have to return those tables. And I want that velvet pillow from the back seat. It's the only thing I have left from my dead grandmother."

Fred promised to drop the tables off at Premiere Party Rents the following day, the day before Thanksgiving. He said he'd leave the pillow at my post office box. I telephoned Rhonda. "My car thief will be returning my tables tomorrow," I chirped.

He didn't. Apparently Fred needed a little nagging. I called an expert: "Mom, you gotta help me out." I coached her on the approach. "You live in a trailer park." "I'm not going to say that!" snipped my middle-class mother. She did, however, manage to lay on the guilt: "Fred, this is Amy's mother. We wanted to have Amy home with us for Thanksgiving, but we couldn't afford to send her a plane ticket, and she couldn't afford to buy one because you stole her car. The least you can do is return those tables. And I can't see what use you could have for that pillow from her grandmother. You return that too! It's the least you can do! That is all!" (That's how my mother ends her phone calls, to daughters and car thieves alike.)

Fred never did return the tables or the pillow. Nor did he make good on his offers to have my car painted or give me his Metro. (I'm still ready to accept.) But he did become a terrific source of free therapy. Whenever I had a bad day, I would call up Fred and rail at him. I even mailed him a nasty letter and a bill for my car-theft-related expenses, addressed to "Fred Lopez, Car Thief." Across the front I wrote, "YOU'RE ROTTEN," "You should be ashamed of yourself!!" On the back I scrawled "I HATE YOU!"

Months went by, and Fred still hadn't been arrested. The case was knocked down to a misdemeanor, which, according to Fesperman, meant the police couldn't go into his house to arrest him. So, it seemed Fred's punishment amounted to being forced to disconnect his phone, probably because he couldn't take the telephone harassment from me and, especially, my mother. Still, I didn't regret the experience. I had great fun moonlighting as a private detective, I encountered some really terrific people—the Rambler nuts and others who went out of their way to help me—and I learned a surprising lesson: In Los Angeles, crime pays. Come to think of it, stealing cars seems like a pretty good way to earn a dishonest living. Unless, of course, you steal my car.

Bran

What I didn't mention when my Rambler story ran in the *Los Angeles Times* is that my mother wasn't the only one I sicced on Fred. In the early '90s, as a struggling writer living in New York, I really couldn't afford to go out, except to parties or gallery openings where the wine was free. I would sometimes join friends at a restaurant, but arrive as the meal was ending, have only a glass of tap water and tip a dollar. This was usually too humiliating, so I'd beg off, invest $1.50 in a big bottle of Diet Coke, and go in for an evening of witty banter in AOL's chat rooms.

Through one of those chat rooms I became friends with this highly literate, very clever and funny eccentric who called himself The Counte—who actually turned out to be Marlon Brando. Like me, Marlon was a big prankster and was always doing magic tricks and playing jokes on people. He especially enjoyed tripping up the Hollyweasels, but anyone who came into range was fair game. Naturally, when my car was stolen, Marlon got right on it.

```
Date:     Friday, November 27, 1998 3:35:40 AM
From:     frangipani@earthlink.net
Subj:     Re: The Wild Turkey Report

NOT GOOD. TELL ME WHAT HIS NAME IS AND OTHER ANCILARY INFO . AND I'LL
CALL HIM MYSELF. ILL MAKE HIM FEEL REAL UNCOMFY REAL FAST. NEED
ADDRESS
AS WELL AND LIST OF HIS PREVIOUS JOBS AND HOW OH FUCK IT ILL JUST
CALL
YOU. IT IS HARD TO REMEMBER THAT THERE IS HELP OUT THERE. DONT DO
SHELL
WORK IF YOU CAN POSSIBLLY OVOID  IT
REMEMBER YOU ARE A CHILD OF THE UNIVERSE AND THAT YOU ARE NOT EVER
UNCONECTED.

                              LOVE
-BRANFLAKES
```

E-mail from Marlon Brando.

Marlon hopped on "the blower," as he sometimes called the telephone, and rang Fred—at 3 A.M., when else? He told Fred it was Marlon Brando, which always unsettled employees at the gas or electric company, let alone a young car thief jolted out of bed in the wee hours. I can't say exactly what he said to Fred, but I know he took his time and said it Godfather-style, and that it started with something like, "She's a nice girl. Why did you take her car?"

Poor Fred. Boosts a car from some goofy girl, and he probably thinks, with all the crime in L.A., who's gonna care? Next thing he knows, he's getting prank-called by Marlon Brando. At that point, I suspect he looked out at my pink Rambler and saw it depreciating fast. After I piled on, with tales of FBI agents dropping out of terrorism task forces to track him down . . . well, what else was there for Fred to do but get this pink nightmare out of his life as soon as he could drive it back to me?

Making Crime Pay ME

Because I had to substitute telephone harassment for police intervention to get my car back, Fred remained on the lam. Meanwhile, a judge issued a bench warrant for him, and the police finally arrested him in a traffic stop. Fred was prosecuted and ordered to pay me $75 restitution every month until he'd compensated me for the stuff he'd removed from my trunk, the damage he'd done to my car, and the financial loss I'd taken on the new transmission I'd just put in. The car would have cost much more to restore than it was worth—money I didn't happen to have. With a heavy heart, I donated it to Goodwill, and, in a panic to have transportation to a freelance job, I ended up buying another aging bad idea on wheels, cheap.

I didn't learn about the restitution order until a year went by and a lady from the City Attorney's office called to ask whether Fred had paid his $75 "this month." "$75 dollars *this month*!?" I said. "That would be $75 more than I've *ever* gotten from Fred."

It was the following year before I heard from the lady again. She told me Fred was in custody, and she again asked if he'd been "keeping up with his payments." Ha. Of course he hadn't! She told me he'd be in court that afternoon (she mentioned that he had "lots of parole violations"—surprise, surprise!), and said if the judge thought Fred wasn't likely to pay, he'd throw him in jail for 180 days *instead*. This was fine by me, except for the "instead" part about the 180 days in jail—meaning he could go to jail *instead* of paying me.

I didn't see why Fred couldn't combine the two. I think of it as "The Hamster Wheel Principle." Let Fred run on a big wheel until he generates enough electricity to pay what he owes me, and his room and board, too, and only then let him out. And shouldn't it be that way for all prisoners? Unfortunately, the government isn't quite the hardass I am, so I figured they'd lock him up someplace with a better TV than I have and let him sleep off his time.

Flash forward to December of 2005. The judge rejiggered the amount of Fred's payments, ordering him to send me $120 a month. For that year's Christmas miracle, Fred actually phoned to tell me that the money would be arriving "on Wednesday." Not surprisingly, Wednesday came and went, and my mailbox remained bare. I called Fred and barked at him, "Fred, Amy Alkon. WHERE'S MY MONEY?!" He claimed to have tracking numbers for a letter overnighted to me, blah blah blah, and would e-mail them to me the next morning "from work." Not surprisingly, my virtual mailbox remained as bare of Fred-mail as my real one.

Luckily, it seems Fred rubbed a few brain cells together, and, well, knock me over with one of those swinging pine tree car deodorizers, that Friday, I got a $600 money order from Fred in the mail. But, Fred's bout of wisdom didn't last. In April 2006, four months after Fred had sent me the $600, I tried to call and e-mail Fred to hit him up for more of what he owed me. The e-mail address and the phone number were both dead. I had a sneaking suspicion Fred was trying to escape me.

I pondered how I might find him, and it occurred to me: "Once a thief, always a thief." I yanked out the last UPS overnight packet he'd sent me. Yes . . . it was from an account—it looked like a business account—probably from a business Fred worked for. Of course, it's possible Fred reimbursed the business for using their account. Possible . . . but unlikely!

I called UPS, got this nice lady with a southern accent on the line, and explained why I was looking for Fred. No fan of car thieves, she was happy to help and gave me the business name, number, and address pronto. I called right away, got Fred on the line, and bitched him out: "Did you think you'd get rid of me? You owe me money! Clearly, I can track you to the ends of the earth, so you'd better just pay up!" And he did: $500 that time.

That's the last check I got from Fred. I haven't gone after him since. The money would be nice, but as much as I like money, I've been lazy about tracking him down again, both because I'm a bit bored with the game of it, and because money was never what the whole thing was about. People shouldn't steal other people's pink cars. Or cars of any color. And if somebody does steal my car or yours, I think they should be tracked down and tormented and I'll do my best to make it happen if I've got the time and the leads.

My Rambler experience made me realize that, while you can't always control whether somebody victimizes you, you can sometimes control whether you remain a victim. Sometimes, you're only a victim because you sit back and accept what's happening to you. This doesn't mean you'll always prevail. But, you at least have to give it a fighting shot.

From the moment I started tracking my Rambler, I found this other side of myself I never realized was there. After that, whenever somebody tried to turn me into their doormat, I leapt into action. In time, I started intervening in small ways for friends and acquaintances I saw being kicked around, doing my best to at least create a little annoyance and unpleasantness for people who'd taken advantage of them. The more I tormented society's petty evildoers, the more comfortable I got doing it, and the more amazed I was that I often seemed able to make a difference. And so I began my second career as "Revengerella," the militant Miss Manners, doing my bit to clobber the world into a kinder, gentler, more considerate place.

4

THE MOBILE SAVAGE

There are people out there who have never been disturbed by some jerk shouting into a cell phone. This guy, for example.

Courtesy of the National Constitution Center, Philadelphia

But, basically, if you're alive, not stone-deaf, and not from a culture where emergency medicine involves running to wake an old guy who wears a bunch of chicken feet around his neck, chances are, you've been bugged half-looney by some boor on a cell phone.

Just go online and skim the reader comments under any article about cell phone rudeness. Everybody's blood-thirsty for cell phone abuser scalp—from bunny-hugging vegans to the ticked-off Noo Yorkuh on the express bus quoted by commenter patsyfromthebronx on nytimes.com. The express bus has a sign discouraging cell phone use, patsy explained, but passengers make allowances for quick, quiet calls to the babysitter. However . . .

> One memorable day when the usual riders were subjected,
> for the umpteenth time, to "HELLO, MA??" ad nauseam, one
> fed-up passenger stood up and yelled "YO, LADY, SHUT
> THE *&^* UP!" and it worked. I love The Bronx.

Some try a more genteel approach. At first, anyway. Metro-North train passenger Carl Zeliger posted this on nytimes.com:

> I once politely asked a person on a cell to lower her
> voice. She noted that she did not like the way I asked
> . . . The result - I screamed at her in a voice that
> scared me and the rest of the car. She did however
> shut up.

Also on nytimes.com, a commenter called Steve posted his solution for when a person in the front of the checkout line is holding everybody up by "jabbering via cell phone":

> I routinely join in the conversation, loudly and
> inappropriately, saying something to the effect of,
> "She'll have to call you back on her own time. Right
> now she's delaying (x) people who want her to shut
> up, pay up, and leave."

Right on, Steve! But, next time, if it's a guy and he sounds like he's talking to his wife, you might try something to the effect of "Jasmine's ready for your lap dance! No touching the strippers this time, buddy. Once more, and you're banned!"

From a techdirt.com blog item, a guy calling himself BTR1701 described getting on the elevator in his apartment building as a woman ran up and stuck her briefcase between the closing doors:

> But she doesn't get on. She just stands there
> holding the doors open and continues her phone
> conversation—because she was afraid if she got
> in the elevator, she'd lose the call. So there she is
> holding the elevator and apparently expecting the
> four of us who were already on it to just stand there
> and wait for her to finish her goddamn phone call.
> . . . Yeah, lady, it's your world. The rest of us are just
> living in it.

People feel free to yap away on cell phones in the most amazing places, like at the doctor's office, and not just in the waiting room. Doug writes on nytimes.com:

> As a physician, I can say without a doubt the most
> egregious use of a cellphone was the female patient
> who answered her telephone while I was in the
> midst of a female pelvic examination . . . a personal
> examination of the visible or palpable internal organs

in a woman and not [like] having your car up on a
rack in the service bay.

Also on nytimes.com, apartment-dweller foggyone complained
about a neighbor who "loves" to sit on the landing between their two
doors and chat away on her cell as late as 10 P.M.:

> I finally appealed to the apartment manager (as did
> several others, because she can be heard a good
> distance away). Asked why she inflicts her private
> life on her neighbors, she said she didn't want to
> disturb her husband. Sigh.

A lot of commenters were steamed about the yahoos who disrupt
movie theater audiences with cell phone conversations and with the
lighted screens of their wireless binkies. Many commenters were in
favor of cell phone jammers—electronic devices, illegal in the U.S.,
that transmit a radio frequency that blocks cell phone signals and ends
or prevents calls. Jammers come in a range of sizes and strengths—
cell phone sized to silence the vulgarian across from you in the dentist's office, or large and powerful enough to civilize entire restaurants
or theaters.

I'm actually against these gizmos because I don't think it's fair to
preemptively punish everybody because some people are rude. Also,
there are those who really do need to be reachable, like parents, doc-
tors on call, and patients waiting for a new liver. I can hear one trans-
plant nurse saying to another: "Whoops, went to voice mail . . . who's
next on the list?"

When some loud cellface takes over a public place, my first course of action is asking politely if they might pipe down a little, or take their call outdoors (it's Southern California, not the northern Yukon). Sometimes, however, I can't manage more than "Shhhhh!" One evening, in the wine aisle at the grocery store Trader Joe's, I was treated to some chick's loud, rapid-fire cellular yammering in what sounded like Korean. I was tired, and she was giving me a companion headache to the headache I'd come in with, so I didn't feel like getting into it with her. Keeping my eyes on the wine, I shushed her. I found this to be an extremely successful tactic—in getting her to remain exactly as loud as before. I shushed louder. This was also extremely effective—in getting the chubby Asian guy with her to get right in my face and yell in heavily accented English, "UP YOU ASS! UP YOU ASS!" It was so sudden and so loud, he could've blown me across the store. Instead, I stood there and weakly informed him that the phone was mobile while the wine aisle was not, grabbed the closest bottle of something white, and dragged what remained of me to the cashier.

The next morning, I was feeling a bit hung over. I'd only had a single glass of wine, but in my haste to escape Kim Jun Pinot Grigio, I guess I'd chosen unwisely. I decided to go to my favorite Venice breakfast spot, the Rose Café. I'd read the paper, listen to the classical music, take in the ocean air and the murmur of quiet conversation, and feel better.

The only problem was . . . seated right next to me, and shouting into a cell phone. After getting hollered at the previous evening, I didn't feel up to instructing yet another adult to "Please use your inside voice!" So, rather conspicuously, or so I thought, I stood up, pulled out a pen and paper, stared straight at the woman on the phone, and began taking notes—my way of shouting without exactly shouting, "HEY, LADY! YOU'RE NOT ALONE!" And I took notes, and took notes, yet she never looked my way. But, as I took notes, she began to look like a blog item, which is what she became:

ANNA STURGESS IS GETTING GLASSES![11]
And she's picking them up Saturday after 4 P.M.!
I know this because she was bellowing into a cell phone about it next to me in a café. Apparently, she's not only inconsiderate, she doesn't seem to mind giving a lot of personal information, starting with her full name, to a total stranger.

She continued, Anna Sturgess and Bob Takamashi "have insurance there," she said . . . "under a flexible spending account." "We just have to pay by the end of the year," she said. And then she most helpfully bellowed her phone number—347-555-5555[12]—*perhaps because she's lonely and wants total strangers to call and ask how her glasses are working out for her.*

Hey, Anna, can I have your bank account number and your login so I can transfer a few bucks to my

---

11 Just like with my car thief, not her real name or her husband's real name. After the story hit *Nightline, The Wall Street Journal,* the *Los Angeles Times,* and the blogosphere, I figured she'd probably learned her lesson.

12 Not her real number. Changed here for the same reason.

account? I'd like to get a pair of noise-canceling headphones in case you sit next to me again.

On a positive note, the little girl with them, probably Anna's (and maybe Bob's) daughter, was very quiet and well behaved.

Hey, Anna, I know it's kinda cold in NYC, where you're apparently from (according to the area code you helpfully dispensed), but here in sunny southern California, at the moment you were talking, it was 58 degrees. Next time, you might take your business outside—as exciting as I found it, on a morning I would normally have relaxed to the classical music while eating my breakfast and thinking my own thoughts, to instead be a part of your eyecare needs.

After the blog item went up, she got calls from around the world—"Anna, your glasses are ready!" Many were thrilled that somebody was finally taking a stand. In my comments section, fellow blogger David Markland called my story "an awesome cautionary tale about why you shouldn't reveal so much personal info in public. And if it keeps assholes from talking loud in a Starbucks, so much the better!"

Others accused me of endangering the lady and her child—silly, since all I did was mention that she had one; not exactly an unusual state of affairs. If you don't want total strangers to know you have children, along with the phone number that leads to you and them, perhaps dispense your number and medical records privately—

someplace where you won't annoy the crap out of a bunch of total strangers.

The truth is, missing children statistics are wildly inflated, according to USC sociologist Barry Glassner. Abductions of children by strangers are actually rather rare. "A total of 200 to 300 a year are abducted by nonfamily members and kept for long periods of time or murdered," writes Glassner in *The Culture of Fear*, citing criminal justice experts. Glassner published his book in 1999, but the myth of extreme stranger danger remains. Most shamelessly, I put it to work the day some lady in a Hollywood Hills Starbucks decided to treat all the other customers there to a command performance of her impromptu spoken-word masterwork, "The Birthday Party Invitation."

The lady made five very loud calls—each the same as the last—giving her name (Carol), detailed directions to a kid's birthday party at her house, plus the time, plus her home phone number. At the Call Number Four mark, other patrons started spilling out of the place, glaring back at her as they left. Carol remained oblivious. I was too far behind in my writing to leave or to even get up and say something to her, but I did scribble down her phone number. I left this message on her voice mail when I got home:

Carol, Carol, Carol . . . the microphone on a cell phone is actually quite sensitive. There's no need to yell. You look like a nice woman. You probably didn't realize that your repeated shouting into your cell phone drove a number of people out of the coffee bar today. Beyond that, you might consider that I'm just one of about 20 people who know that you live at "555 Ferngrove Street,"[13] a half-block off Sunset, three houses from the end on the right side, and that you're having a bunch of six-year-olds over at 3 P.M. on Saturday. Now, I'm just a newspaper columnist, not a pedophile, but it's kind of an unnecessary security risk you're taking, huh? Just a little something to think about the next time you're shouting on your cell phone in a coffee bar. Bye!

Whenever I blog stuff like this, at least a commenter or two wants to know who crowned me the arbiter of public cell phone manners. Janet was one of them:

Get over yourself. You were in a public place, and in public, one overhears other people talking. What difference should it make if the conversation was on a cell phone or to a tablemate?

Excellent question, Janet. It was a public place—which seems a pretty good argument for not seizing all the available airspace, either with your cell phone conversation or by standing up and announcing, "Ladies and gentlemen, I will now read aloud from the tax code! Or, would you prefer some original free verse?"

Regarding Janet's other point, let's say somebody on a cell phone isn't shouting, just talking. What's it matter whether they're chatting with somebody seated across from them, or with somebody seated

---

13 No, of course it's not her real address!

across the country? Actually, research seems to indicate that other people's cell phone conversations are especially invasive because you're missing half of what's being said, and that seems to be a real problem for your brain.

A paper published in 2004 by York University's Dr. Andrew Monk and his colleagues showed that one-sided conversations are more intrusive and annoying—whether the person talking is on a cell phone, or talking with another person whose side of the conversation isn't audible. It's likely your brain is compelled to pay attention and fill in the side of the conversation you can't hear. Dr. Mark Liberman, a University of Pennsylvania linguist, speculates that, after a few seconds of hearing half a conversation, the front part of your brain, the chief-executive/decision-making area, "is throbbing like a stubbed toe. Or at least it's interfering with your ability to think about other things."

Liberman believes this mind-jacking is a side effect of the human capacity for mind reading—not swami-in-a-jeweled-turban-style, but in the little ways we all do, all day, every day, to predict what other people are thinking and feeling, and in turn, how they'll behave. This ability, called "Theory of Mind," is how, when somebody's shaking his fist at you and growing increasingly red-faced, you can be reasonably sure he's angry, not gleefully happy, and is more likely to end up clocking you one than hugging you. Humans not only have an *ability* for mind reading, "It's . . . pretty much automatic," Liberman writes. ". . . You can't stop yourself from reading your companions' minds any more than you can stop yourself from noticing the color of their clothes. But when you're only getting half the cues—from one side of a cell phone conversation between two strangers—you have to work a lot harder."

That's why even the cell phone conversations of people trying to speak in a low tone can be intrusive. Since I know that few people know this, I give them points for making an effort. But, even now, I'm always a little mystified at how so many public cell phoners belt it out like they aren't just talking to one person on the other end but like they actually intend to send a message to the entire restaurant: "I'M NOT WEARING ANY PANTIES!" (Uh, thanks for sharing . . . mister.)

Part of the problem, says Northwestern University professor and product design guru Don Norman, is that cell phones lack something called "sidetone." Norman, who draws from engineering and cognitive science to improve product usability, explains that sidetone is a technological innovation from the early days of the telephone, in which sound going into the mouthpiece of the phone is fed back into the earpiece. He explains that "speaking level is determined, in part, by auditory feedback—how loudly one hears their own voice." In the absence of sidetone, people aren't aware of just how loud they are.

Norman believes sidetone was eliminated from mobile phones for two reasons: First, "modern telephonic engineers have no sense of history," and aren't clued in to the reasons behind the development of sidetone feedback. And second, it poses more difficult problems in the environments the cell phone is used in, "where wind noise on the microphone and high levels of ambient noise pose technical limitations on sidetone."

Norman says—and I agree—that it's time to bring sidetone back. "Certainly with today's noise-filtering technology, we could cancel natural background noises." He, like me, sees other solutions as well. He suggests developing "voice cups" to shield the speaker's voice from external listeners. I suggest developing nostalgia—for the old days of phone booths in the back of restaurants. Self-important jerks who just *must* make that call (to their answering machine at home)—"Buy low! Sell high!"—could be ushered to the back to a set of two or three enclosed Lucite phone cones, keeping them from keeping you from being heard as you're trying to have a quiet conversation with your date.

In the meantime, I suggest asking restaurants, cafés, and other businesses you patronize to put up NO CELL PHONES signs. Here's one from Just Tantau, an artsy-craftsy jewelry and gift store in Venice, California:

Please don't use this store as a phone booth unless your name is Clark Kent.

The sign on the door at Just Tantau.

Of course, store and restaurant cell phone bans are worthless if they aren't enforced. In fact, every time somebody gets away with jawing on their cell phone, the rule against it gets degraded—until it's eventually just a meek suggestion. Knowing that, when the staff at my favorite "no cell phones" café is busy, and some lout is yammering away, I'll always say something: "Excuse me, they have a no cell phones policy here. They ask that you take your calls outside."

Some people thank me for telling them and continue their call outside. Others offer excuses for why the "no cell phones" rule shouldn't apply to them. "I'm talking to my son!" one woman snapped. I thought it, but didn't say it: *I don't care if it's Jesus, and you're making travel arrangements for his return.* I calmly and politely pointed out to the lady that the "no cell phones" policy was intended to be broadly applied (as in, it wasn't meant for everyone in the entire universe but her). "Take some Prozac!" she barked. Finally, I couldn't help myself. I chirped, "Because my taking Prozac will cure you of your bad manners?"

As you can see, trying to make the world a less noise-polluted place is no way to win popularity contests. In fact, as I mentioned in Chapter 1, people are quick to think *you're* the jerk for speaking up—even if they're being bothered, too—because there's a tendency to confuse asking some hee-hawing cellface to keep it down with impinging on that person's freedom. I wasn't quite sure how to get around this misperception, so I turned to Dr. Pat Barclay, a researcher at Cornell who studies altruism and costly punishment. "People would need to realize that the behavior that is being punished is detrimental to everybody else," Barclay explained. "Otherwise, the punishment just appears to be mean."

I realized that I first needed to get people in a given environment to understand that their attention is a valuable resource, and then, that the loud jerk on the cell phone is taking more than his or her fair share of a public space, stealing from everyone else in it. I wasn't quite sure how to communicate all that, short of passing out annotated copies of "The Tragedy of the Commons" to people in line at the drugstore and standing over them with a metal ruler as they read it.

But, maybe I was overcomplicating things. Maybe I just needed to help people realize they're being screwed over by all the loud cell phoners. It occurred to me that I might be able to do that by changing just one word of a message I often use on ornery cell shouters.

Instead of telling them "MY attention doesn't belong to you," I should say "OUR attention doesn't belong to you." In other words, I'm not just speaking up for my own peace of mind, but for the good of the group—for everybody who prefers hearing their friend's funny story or their own thoughts to some mobile narcissist's loud battle to get a refund on his health club membership.

I was eager to try my theory out. I didn't have long to wait. I'd interviewed Barclay at the NEEPS (NorthEastern Evolutionary Psychology Society) conference in Manchester, New Hampshire. In the Manchester airport, waiting to fly home, I sat down in the only empty seat in a block of six. Four seats down, a chubby, curly-haired man, about 50, started bellowing into his phone, and kept bellowing, repeatedly disparaging some colleague he mentioned by first and last name. Hilariously, he informed the person on the other end, "This is not for publication." Oh, isn't it?

I shushed the guy (from down the row, to no avail), and the guy next to me kept putting his book down and making loud sighs of frustration (also to no avail). Finally, I'd had it. I stood up, planted myself front and center before the row of seats, about three feet from the guy, and said to him, "Excuse me, but why do you think OUR attention belongs to you?"

The guy and others in the row looked up at me with surprise. I was on a roll. "If you're going to carry on a loud conversation," I continued, "why do you think it's appropriate to do it in the middle of all these people who are forced to listen to you?"

The guy, still on the phone, responded, "I'm just talking to a friend." (Yeah, don't tell me . . . a Mr. J.H. Christ?)

"We shouldn't be forced to listen to you do a monologue on your life," I said.

Nobody else spoke up. But, on the bright side, nobody else spoke up against me for speaking up, either. Maybe I was on to something. Pointing to an unoccupied area by a stairway, I said to the guy, "I went over there to talk on my cell phone because I didn't want to disturb anyone. I know, novel concept."

"I'll go to the other side of the airport for you," he said, agitated.

"It's not for me," I said. "It's common etiquette." (Well, okay, increasingly uncommon etiquette, but I hope to change that.)

The guy rolled his eyes and stomped off. And, it's a good thing he did—before I got around to taking notes on the "not for publication" portion of his conversation. That's what I did on an L.A.-to-San Francisco flight when the blowhard seated behind me was bellowing into his phone, in detail, about a top-secret $3 million insurance deal he was doing. That guy said something along the lines of "If anyone finds out about this before Monday, we're sunk."

I grinned. I won't tell a soul, I thought. Well, except for a few people on the World Wide Web.[14]

Over time, in my attempts to put a damper on the cell shouters, I've found incorporating "we," "us," and "our" to be surprisingly effective.

---

14 Lucky him, I was busy all weekend at a newspaper conference, and never got around to blogging it.

When I make it clear that I'm speaking out on behalf of the group, the rudester tends to seem a little more chastened, and fellow sufferers often thank me. (Occasionally, people clap.)

Of course, there are times when the group defense tactic doesn't fit the bill, like early one morning at the "no cell phones" café when there were only two of us in the place: yours truly and the woman directly behind me, clucking like a mad hen into her phone. I leaned around the back of my booth and said, "Excuse me, there's a no cell phones policy here."

She glared at me. "I'm on the phone! You're interrupting my call!"

"And you're interrupting my life. With mental litter." I pointed out the "no cell phones" sign, and suggested she go outside to talk on her cell (instead of doing it six inches from the back of my head).

The woman, a neo-hippie by way of Neiman Marcus, took another brief break from her call to tell me how rude I was and strode out the door.

Upon her return, she lectured me on the terrible damage I was doing to my "karma." Yeah, uh-huh, whatever. "My time is worth something," I said to her. "And you stole 30 seconds of my attention."

Surely intending to insult me, she said, "Here, I'll give you a dollar!"

"Okay! Cool!" I said. And I meant it. If you're willing to pay me for the time you take from me, you're not stealing from me, you're employing me. I waited, smiling, as she dug in her purse. It turned out she only had a 20.

"I have to get change!" she snarled.

"Okay!" I chirped, smiling at her.

She didn't like my attitude one bit. I'm guessing I was supposed to brim with shame and decline her offer of filthy lucre. Sorry, yogacheeks, I'm a capitalist, and time is money. And, now, thanks to you, my going rate for listening to dull conversations that have nothing to do with me is $120 an hour ($1 for every 30 seconds of tedium).

I took a picture of the dollar she gave me. George, to his credit, seems to be looking disapprovingly back in her direction.

Dollar on the table at the no cell phones café.

There are those who will absolutely refuse to pipe down. They can at least be given an earful of their own medicine (use discretion, lest a rudester be armed with more than a RAZR). A guy in the pen aisle at Staples decided I would be an appropriate audience for his loud argument with his girlfriend—until my loud, dramatic recitation of my to-do list made it a little hard for him to hear himself putting her down. (Of course, avoid doing this sort of thing if any other customers are anywhere near you.)

When somebody next to me in a café refuses to stop yakking my ear off, I like to read aloud at commensurate volume from my book or newspaper; for example, a passage from behavioral ecologist Marlene Zuk's very entertaining *Riddled with Life* that starts "I came to a fondness for chickens late in life. . . ." Whatever you're reading from is probably about 10 times more interesting than whatever they were saying. Unfortunately, the wireless ill-mannered are always the last to see the benefits of an information meritocracy, so I prepared a message they can take home for further study (feel free to photocopy it and hand it out to the loud perp nearest you):

**IF YOU CAN READ THIS CARD
YOU ARE TOO LOUD**

Just because you have a self doesn't mean you should express it. Apparently, you are under the impression that the world will be a better place once you broadcast the news that you've changed laxatives or forgotten to floss. Perhaps you call this "freedom of speech." I call it "bad breeding." Kindly save your loud, dull conversations for the privacy of your home. Thank you!

Now, I do understand that there are times people in a public place just can't help but make a quick call. Gotta remind the babysitter that little Cody isn't allowed to smoke crack before dinner? Like the express bus riders patsyfromthebronx described, I'll do my best to deal. In all other cases, here are the two guidelines I suggest for public cell phoning etiquette:

1. Public cell phone calls are fine as long as one is talking at a decibel level just this side of a whisper; preferably with one's hand cupped over one's mouth.
2. Otherwise, one shouldn't use a cell phone anywhere one wouldn't feel perfectly comfortable passing a big, loud cloud of gas.

5

THE BUSINESS OF BEING RUDE, PART 1

I was a loser as a child. I had no friends until I was midway through my teens, so I spent my entire childhood escaping in books. Once, I even crashed into a parked car as I was reading while riding my bike. I don't remember the details of the stories I mowed through, just the more compelling characters: Nancy Drew, Tom Swift, Ozma of Oz, Harriet the Spy, Mrs. Basil E. Frankweiler, and when I was really young, Goofus and Gallant, from a monthly children's magazine everyone's dentist used to get called *Highlights for Children*.

Goofus and Gallant are the two boys in a little morality comic that's been in the magazine since the 1940s. Goofus is the lazy, selfish brat who does whatever he can get away with. Gallant is the good boy, kind and generous, always looking out for others. Fast forward 20 years, and you can picture Gallant joining the Peace Corps and singlehandedly laying 10 miles of pipe through rocky desert to bring fresh water to some remote village. Goofus, meanwhile, is pleading out on a purse-snatching charge.

Courtesy of *Highlights for Children*

Looking at these strips now, I can see Goofus as a bit of an icono-clast. (My boyfriend called him "misunderstood.")

Courtesy of *Highlights for Children*

But, all in all, *Goofus and Gallant*® reminds me how doing the right thing usually comes down to simple stuff you were supposed to learn when you were a kid:[15]

---

15 *All I Really Need to Know I Learned in Kindergarten*, Robert Fulghum (Villard, 1988).

- ▸ Play fair.
- ▸ Don't hit people.
- ▸ Clean up your own mess.
- ▸ Don't take things that aren't yours.
- ▸ Say you're sorry when you hurt somebody.
- ▸ Flush.

That same thinking actually applies to business, and this is a tale of two businesses—the Goofus and the Gallant.

Goofus, Inc.

Protecting customer information is a top priority at B of A and we have multiple layers of security.

—Bank of America spokeslady Betty Riess[16]

While I'd like readers of my newspaper column to picture me spending afternoons in a silk dressing gown in a canopy bed dotting witticisms on vellum with a big lavender quill pen, the reality of my writing process is somewhat different: long sweaty hours spent crawling under furniture looking for better verbs while dolled up in decaying workout wear by Karl TheLimitederfeld and Yves St. The Gap.

One Tuesday, I was about two hours from my deadline and about three hours from a funny and coherent final paragraph when the phone rang. Grrr. The woman on the other end said she was calling from Bank of America—probably to try to sell me some account-enhancing crap in the middle of my hell day. But, she didn't launch

---

16 Wired.com blog post by Ryan Singel, February 27, 2008.

into a sales pitch. She asked whether I'd "noticed any fraud" on my account. Fraud on my account?! Eeek! "Hold on!" I said. I pulled up my Web browser, typed in bankofamerica.com, and began the login process.

There had to be some mistake. I am, let's just say, a little loonytunes about safeguarding my personal and financial data. I won't use a debit card. I rarely write checks, and then only to the IRS, my auto insurer, and a few trusted people I've known for years, as I consider checks risky instruments. (Why not just hand out business cards imprinted with your bank account number?) I pay for almost everything, including my phone bill, on a single credit card (contrary to popular belief, a very safe way to transact). I'm so security conscious that in 2005, way before identity theft was so much in the public eye, I put a "security freeze"[17] on my credit bureau accounts, meaning nobody can get credit in my name without "thawing" my accounts with a PIN possessed only by me.

Naturally, I have the Lamborghini of shredders—which I mostly use on reader e-mail. I don't shred important personal or financial documents; I store them, decades of them. After all, I watch "CSI"—somewhere out there, there's some hot blonde with movie-star looks and a big magnifying glass who can piece these things back together. If ever I make a mistake writing a check, I write VOID all over it and black out my name and address with a big permanent magic marker. I will shred it—but only after I rip off the account number, burn it in a little steel dish in my sink, and flush the ashes down the toilet.

---

17 U.S. residents should Google "security freeze," plus their state name, and seriously consider doing this.

In other words, I'm not the kind of person who gets money hacked out of her— "OH MY GOD!" I said to the woman on the phone. "There's *a lot* of money missing! Like, thousands and thousands of dollars!"

The woman was Debbie, the associate manager from the Dixon City, California, branch of Bank of America, about 20 miles from Sacramento, and about 400 miles from me. On Friday, one of Debbie's tellers had dispensed $1,500 from my checking account to some woman who was not me—a woman with *only* a fake driver's license in my name . . . with the wrong expiration date!

After collecting the $1,500 from my checking, the thief sidled over to the next teller to defoliate my savings. When that teller asked to see her driver's license, "that's when we noticed that the expiration date was different," Debbie claimed.[18] She said the woman then said, "Maybe I'll write a check for the down payment," and left the bank.

Other than the incorrect expiration date, Debbie told me the woman's fake license had my real information, down to my actual driver's license number. I was stunned. How could this woman have gotten my account numbers, let alone a driver's license in my name and state-issued number? I asked Debbie if she'd seen the thief. She had. "What did she look like?" I asked.

Debbie described her: "An African-American, woman, heavy . . . teeth missing in front."

Excuse me? Forget the fact that I'm the color of fresh Wite-Out, with bright red hair. But, missing teeth? Missing teeth?! What kind

---

18 I have my doubts as to whether they actually "noticed" anything on Friday, since it took them until Tuesday afternoon to get in touch with me.

of person in this day and age goes around with missing teeth?! I posed this question to Debbie: "Sorry, but you see missing teeth, and do you think hardworking girl with a chunk of money in the bank . . . or . . . CRACK WHORE?!"

Debbie's response? "We don't like to judge people."

Oh, don't you? Well, how about this, Debs? When it's your money, go right ahead and leave the judgment by the wayside. When it's my money . . . ASK LOTS AND LOTS OF QUESTIONS!

Debbie's teller was just one of a bunch of B of A tellers who'd handed over my money without verifying who they were giving it to. Seven times in a single statement period, Bank of America's tellers dispensed $12,000 of my money to thieves (one in Texas and one in the middle of California). These thieves presented ONLY a fake driver's license in my name, with the wrong expiration date. No PIN was required. No bank card was demanded. The signature was not verified. Seven times.

While B of A's tellers were loath to bother my thieves with a lot of prying questions—okay, *any* prying questions—the bank had stopped just short of waterboarding me when I'd tried to put money INTO my IRA the previous year. And it's not like I dropped by a branch with a big chest of gold doubloons or a banker box marked "DRUG PROFITS." I called up Bank of America and asked to transfer some middle-class-meager sum from my checking or savings to my IRA. Their guy agreed to make the transfer—only a few thousand dollars—only after he interrogated me to be sure I really was Amy Alkon, not, say, some really dim criminal who goes around putting thousands of dollars into unwitting customers' retirement accounts.

Of course, I bent over like a good girl and gave the guy every-thing he needed—momma's blood type, dead grandma's elementary school home room. It wasn't enough. About 20 days after I *thought* I'd deposited the money into my IRA, I got a letter from Bank of America informing me that they were unable to make the deposit. I called their toll-free number (free in phone bill terms, emotionally costly). According to their phone rep, because I had a credit freeze, they weren't able to accept my deposit over the phone; I had to go to my branch. It was a pain, but I wasn't about to unfreeze my credit.[19]

I kept wondering, with all I went through in order to put a rel-atively small sum of money *into* the bank, how were these thieves able to basically present a piece of used Kleenex with my name on it and have the teller hand over piles of my money? I asked Debbie: when Old Toothless asked for my money, did they look at the com-puter to verify whether she was me . . . check the signature and all? Debbie got a funny sound in her voice. She told me they "couldn't access" the computer. Great. Fantastic time to have a computer glitch, I thought.

Even so, the thief was a woman with a piece of ID that banks know (hell, even I know) is easily faked. I could go down to L.A.'s MacArthur Park right now, hand over $150, and get a fake California driver's license in anybody's name: Angelina Jolie, Cruella De Vil, Your Name. Yet, Debbie and her colleagues didn't so much as make a 37-cent long-distance call to my branch in Los Angeles, didn't ask to

---

19 And what were they doing, anyway, nosing around in my credit reports because I transferred a few thousand dollars of my own money to a retirement savings account?

have my signature faxed to them. Nope, they just smiled and handed over $1,500 of my money.

I was furious, but I couldn't waste time dwelling on the bank's mistakes. The theft had been caught in under a month, meaning I'd get my money back,[20] so I was laser-focused on just one thing: Catching the thieves running around with a fake driver's license in my name. I'd already tracked down one car thief, I told Debbie, and I was pretty confident I could track these creeps down, too. All I would need was the videotape of the thief from her bank.

Uh, sorry, Debbie told me. No go. "Privacy," she explained.

"Privacy?" I said, not quite getting it. "Wait. You mean privacy . . . *for the thief*?!"

That's exactly what she meant.

And so began my battle with B of A. I was determined to track down the thieves. Bank of America was determined to stop me.

It's my understanding that you're more likely to catch a criminal if you go after them soon after a crime is committed. That's why that reality show about homicide detectives is called "The First 48." As the opening voiceover explains, "For homicide detectives, the clock starts ticking the moment they are called. Their chance of solving a case is cut in half if they don't get a lead in the first 48 [hours]."

As soon as I made my column deadline, I ran to the bank and got my checking and savings accounts closed and reopened with new

---

20 A B of A employee told me I had 90 days from the receipt of a bank statement showing theft to report it and be assured of getting money back.

account numbers. Next, I sped to the police station to make a report, but there was a problem. No letter of fraud from the bank, no can do, the desk officer informed me.

The next morning, Wednesday, May 28, I got on the phone to get the fraud letter from B of A—in between making dozens of extremely upsetting "I'm an identity theft victim!" cleanup calls to the DMV, the credit bureaus, and myriad other institutions with "press one if you'd like to kill yourself with pills; press two if you'd like to hang yourself" phone trees.

Now, considering that B of A associate manager Debbie from Dixon had seen the thief, an African-American woman with some serious dental issues, and given that a quick Web search would verify that I'm neither African-American nor missing any teeth, you'd think B of A would front me that letter. Just some little fax saying I'd been robbed. You know, in the spirit of wanting to get the thief in a timely manner. Three words kept coming to me: They. Don't. Care.

Whenever I pressed enough buttons to get through to a live person in B of A's L.A.-based fraud claims unit (they cleverly demur from giving you direct phone numbers), I explained again and again why it was important that they send me the fraud letter fast. In addition to repeatedly making the "First 48" point, I told them I'd called the Dixon City police department first thing that morning in hopes of getting them looking for the thief. The front-toothless woman had not only violated my account there, but in nearby Auburn.

Now there are 311 black people in Dixon City, and 84 in Auburn. (I looked it up.) How hard can it be to find one gap-mouthed 40-something black lady in the area—I mean, if you do it in a timely manner? The Dixon City officer I spoke to said she was very sorry, but

I'd need a letter from the bank saying I'd been a victim of fraud . . . in order to get a police report from my local L.A. precinct . . . in order for their department to proceed with any investigation.

I tried to persuade the fraud department reps that I'm not a typical victim; that I actually have a chance of catching the thief. I have investigative skills from reporting, and I'd already used them to track down one car thief and a hit-and-run driver, both of whom were prosecuted, thanks to me. So . . . that fraud letter, please? Pretty please with a fake driver's license on top?

The more I batted up against B of A's fraud claims drones, the angrier I got. Sure, they've got bodies there manning the phone lines, but even a woman who said she was a VP was unable to expedite matters—and never mind that it made it less likely that a fraudster would be caught. Bureaucracy rules, justice drools!

B of A's letter attesting to the fraud they'd apparently discovered on Tuesday finally came by fax and e-mail on Friday—just in time for me to make a police report that would gather dust all weekend. They also returned my stolen money, as I knew they would. My stolen peace of mind wasn't so easily credited back. As for my time they'd sucked, first due to their stunningly lax security, and then with their stonewalling, who'd reimburse me for that?

Meanwhile, I was becoming something of a problem victim— one with the reportorial skills to track down the honchos at B of A who don't normally talk to the dirty, icky consumers. "And when will Mr. Mayopoulos return?" I asked the annoyed assistant to B of A general counsel Timothy Mayopoulos. Shortly afterward, I got kicked over to the oddly named Nereida Claudius,[21] whose letters announced her as "VP; Customer Advocate, Office of the Chairman." Cool. Somebody with some clout was going to help me. (Uh, think again, Ames.)

Claudius, with her slow, soft, methodical way of speaking, is a vocal ringer for Republican speechwriter-turned-pundit Peggy Noonan. Like Noonan, she sounds like a cross between a first-grade teacher and somebody who deals with a lot of slow-witted psychotics. You can get a pretty good sense of her from her soothingly irritating corporatese in this letter she sent me June 5:

> Dear Ms. Alkon,
> Thank you for your electronic communications regarding the recent activity on your accounts. Representing Bank of America, and as a Customer Advocate in the Office of the Chairman, I consider it a privilege to be able to respond and address your concerns.

"And do absolutely nothing about them," she somehow neglected to add.

Next, she went into a little more detail on exactly what they wouldn't be doing for me:

---

21 Claudius is the Roman dude who took over after they offed Caligula. Nereida means "sea nymph." It is also a bacteria genus.

> Although I must respectfully decline your personal request
> for any available photos of the alleged perpetrators,
> please allow me to assure you that Bank of America will
> fully cooperate with any investigation you choose to pursue
> through law enforcement channels.

Well, there's some fantastic news! Bank of America will be cooperating with an investigation that will probably never take place. The bank knows full well that law enforcement agencies have neither the time nor the resources to pursue claims like mine in any substantive way—if at all. The LAPD pursues only the tiniest fraction of the veritable mountain range of identity theft cases they get. When I called on June 11, the LAPD fraud unit hadn't even opened my report. Yet, Claudius had just informed me that their investigators were "working with the police." Really? Since my case hadn't even been glanced at, what were they all working on, centerpiece arrangements for the policemen's ball?

Chances are, the LAPD only ended up sending my case out to the local departments in Texas and Auburn and Dixon City, California, because I knew to call and "sell them" my case. I had a detective in another LAPD unit coach me on how I might persuade the fraud unit detective that mine was a case worth pursuing: "This is one of the solvable ones! I'm not your ordinary victim! I've already done all this legwork, and I'll do plenty more!"

The bank's fraud investigators were also unlikely to devote much in the way of resources to one $12,000 loss when, in my branch alone, the woman who closed and reopened my account told me she takes the report of an identity theft victim like me every day. I knew there was nobody out there—no busy cop, no hired hand for the bank—who'd care like I did about getting the thief. I was chomping at the bit to drive up to Auburn and Dixon City to get leads and put up wanted posters. I didn't tell B of A this, but I also had an idea for video wanted posters: a plan to put the tape of each thief up on YouTube as a little music video with a catchy soundtrack and a reward offer.

I kept begging Claudius and others at B of A: Please . . . the bank's negligence has caused me immeasurable harm . . . just give me that tape and I'll track these women down—women who surely had others' IDs; others who hadn't known to freeze their credit bureau accounts like I had. I would be glad to sign something—some legal statement absolving the bank of any responsibility, if that's what they were worried about.

Of course, I never knew what they were worried about, if anything, because they would never explain why they were refusing me the tape, just that I couldn't have it, despite the fact that they owed it to me by law.[22] The more I sought to protect myself and others from future damage, the more they shut me down. In fact, Claudius eventually told me she would be the only bank employee allowed to communicate with me, and she would only communicate in writing, no phone calls.

---

22 So lawyer and identity theft expert Mari Frank told me, and it's right there on the FTC's website: "By law, companies must give you a copy of the application or other business transaction records relating to your identity theft." (www.ftc.gov/bcp/edu/pubs/consumer/idtheft/idt04.shtm)

Around then, my situation went from worse to even worse. I opened a letter from Target, and found that the thieves weren't satisfied just cleaning out my bank accounts:

Dear Amy B. Alkon:

Thanks for your interest in a Target Credit Card. We're sorry, but we had to stop processing your application because when we tried to verify your credit history with the credit bureau(s) listed below, it looked like you'd placed a security freeze on your credit report. We can continue working on your application, but first we need you to un-freeze your report and then call or write us to let us know.

I felt like the lady in *The Wizard of Oz* who had the house dropped on her. There were more letters like this to come—from Sears, Kmart, Wal-Mart, and another from Target—all attempts to get instant credit in my name; probably to buy widescreen TVs and the like to pawn or sell on eBay. Horrified, I realized the thieves had my Social Security number.

I spent another whole day calling credit bureaus, putting a password on every credit card I have, and calling every company I have ever had a credit card with, plus a bunch of department stores I thought they might've tried. Most upsettingly, when I called Macy's, I learned that one of the thieves had tried to reopen my recently closed account, but couldn't answer a series of security questions they'd asked, so Macy's turned her down. (Yay, Macy's!)

Now, the way some people have a talent for soccer or ballroom dancing, I'm talented at sleeping. I can actually nap on demand—put my head down and catch three minutes of sleep, anytime, anywhere, as long as I have a flat surface (and a pair of earplugs if it's especially noisy). But, before long, I had difficulty getting to sleep at any hour, and I'd wake up in the middle of the night besieged with worry. When would one of these thieves rent an apartment in my name or open a utility account? All it would take would be a landlord or utility that didn't run a credit check.

Even worse, there was the warning Chris Hoofnagle, an information privacy researcher at UC Berkeley Law, e-mailed me—reminding me that, from now on, I'm at risk for arrest for crimes committed by someone with an ID in my name. Lawyer and identity theft expert[23] Mari Frank advises identity theft victims to run a criminal background check on themselves at least once a year to find out whether anybody has, for example, been arrested for murder in their name. That happened to one of her clients when his Social Security number was mixed up with another Social Security number—even though the name attached to the arrest wasn't his. Frank told "Frontline," "He had no idea for two years that there was a murder arrest *[on his record]* and he couldn't get a job."

When I wasn't imagining myself being beaten senseless in jail after being wrongfully arrested for liquor store holdups by my toothless doppelganger, I'd bolt up in the middle of the night wondering what other information the thieves might have; like, whether they

---

23 I recommend Mari Frank's terrific book, *From Victim to Victor: A Step-by-Step Guide for Ending the Nightmare of Identity Theft,* which contains not only detailed instructions, but a CD with all the letters you'll need to send to credit bureaus, etc., written by a lawyer.

knew my PIN number—the same PIN still attached to my checking and savings—and whether the thieves had tried to imitate my rather unique and sweeping signature. (This would mean the thieves had access to more than just the number on my driver's license, and that they'd have the power to violate me in situations where a signature is used for verification.) Again and again I e-mailed Claudius, begging for details on how deep the breach went. Claudius almost always took her sweet time in answering—sometimes weeks—that is, when she answered at all.

Claudius did FedEx me one pretty shocking communication—a letter informing me that the bank was firing me as a customer—apparently because I'd complained a little too bitterly that they'd failed in their fiduciary[24] duty to me. Now, I'm not an idiot. I'd planned to move my money—but at my convenience, not theirs.[25] Admittedly, it probably didn't help that I'd informed B of A chairman Kenneth D. Lewis of what I'd been going through by faxing him my blog item "Bank Of America Customer? Bury Your Money In A Mason Jar In The Backyard Instead."

Fired from my bank and still videotapeless, I turned my attention to how the thieves could've gotten my driver's license and bank account details. Although I won't shop at a store that requires me to show my

---

24 A lawyer described this to me as the very substantial duty a financial institution has to guard customers' money and personal data.

25 The identity theft happened two months before my book was due, and I was working day and night to make my deadline, and told Claudius so.

driver's license to pay with my credit card, there was no getting around two institutions keeping my driver's license on file: the DMV and my auto insurer. A DMV fraud investigator looked at their records and told me nobody had applied for a new or replacement license in my name, meaning the license the thieves had was a fake. A second DMV fraud investigator explained that the DMV doesn't have my bank account number, and while they do have my Social Security number, it was locked deep in their records, and would be accessible only to the likes of DMV fraud investigators, not to ordinary employees. It was the same at my auto insurer, a manager there told me.

So, how did the thieves get this info combo platter? My driver's license number *and* the personal information on my license *and* my bank account number *and* my Social Security number? There was only one institution that had all four, and that was the bank. On April 2, just 12 days before the thefts began, I'd dutifully dragged myself to my branch to deposit money into my IRA. A woman I'll call Pauline, the same woman who'd closed and reopened my account after the thefts, processed my transaction. At one point, she asked me for my driver's license number, which I grudgingly gave her— although I found out later from a B of A Web page that it was not bank policy to ask for it under these circumstances, as I was (1) a longtime bank customer, and (2) doing an in-bank transaction for a sum under $10,000.

I remembered something identity theft lawyer Mari Frank told me, per the Orange County Attorney—that 60 to 70 percent of identity theft cases start with a "dirty insider." I must emphasize, I have no proof of any wrongdoing at my branch, but I had read of cases where gang members approached bank employees and pressured them to give up information, and where bank employees sold customer information for mere pocket change. I e-mailed Claudius demanding to know whether the bank had investigated the employees at my branch, and any employees who'd accessed my account electronically. She gave the exact same response she gave to so many of my questions— none whatsoever. Luckily, I still had a previous communication from Claudius to cling to—the one in which she wrote that they "consider this matter closed."

Well, how lovely for them!

For 29 years, my boyfriend Gregg has been the researcher for "the poet laureate of wild assholes with guns," the Detroit-based crime novelist Elmore Leonard. In early July of 2008, Gregg was in Detroit, and instead of waiting to deposit his paycheck at his Los Angeles B of A, he went to a branch near his mom's house. It was a former LaSalle Bank, a Midwestern chain acquired by B of A in October 2007.

Before making his deposit, he double-checked with the teller—B of A would clear his check right away, same as always, right? Uh, actually, the teller told him, it would take an extra day to clear because . . . their Bank of America branch *wouldn't be online with Bank of America's computers until October 2008.*

When my boyfriend tossed off this information to me in a bit of morning venting, Debbie from Dixon City's voice played back in my head—that funny strained sound she got when she told me they "couldn't access" the computer to verify whether it was actually me. Little black clouds of suspicion started gathering in my mind: *Seven times* Bank of America's tellers had neglected to do the most rudimentary checking on the bank's computers—like pulling up my signature and comparing it to that of the person presenting only a driver's license in my name and asking for thousands of dollars in cash.

One teller, maybe even two, failing to check—I can chalk that up to routine sloppiness, random error, or a bad hangover. But, SEVEN tellers, all equally negligent, suggest that not verifying ID isn't an accident, but *procedure*. What bank—especially what major, national bank—would make it their procedure to hand their customers' money over to anyone presenting a single piece of easily counterfeited ID?

For answers, I turned to a lawyer for a large bank chain in the South. When I told her how B of A had allowed my account to be violated repeatedly by thieves with only the flimsiest bit of fake ID, she was shocked. "There's no basic fraud detection system at work here," she said. At her bank, if a customer isn't a longtime client a teller knows, the teller will call up an image file of the customer's signature on the bank's computer, or, if that can't be accessed, pull up a cancelled check. The signature image takes about 30 seconds to access, she told me, as opposed to about two minutes for a canceled check—not exactly terribly time- or labor-intensive.

She said her bank might not give serious scrutiny the first time a customer withdraws a large sum of cash, but the second time, the account would be electronically flagged. Off-pattern withdrawals would also be flagged—for example, the five $1,000-plus withdrawals by my thieves in a single day at various teller windows in places I've never been in Texas—when I almost never go to teller windows, and only withdraw about $200 a month from one of several ATMs within a few miles of my Los Angeles house.

I asked friends and family members to test security measures at their banks. My sister, for example, went to a Wells Fargo branch a few miles from her house with only her driver's license and tried to withdraw money from her account. They apologized profusely, but said she'd have to have her ATM card with her and punch in her PIN. Others who bank at WaMu and other institutions gave me similar reports. And sure, there will always be instances where individual tellers are negligent, but at no bank besides B of A did negligence seem to be standard operating procedure.

I decided to test Bank of America's security myself. Naturally, my plan called for a disguise—a $9.99 wig I'd bought on 14th Street in New York that I thought made me look like a Chinese hooker.

Me, bewigged.

I'd go down to MacArthur Park and buy a fake ID—in my own real name and driver's license number, but with the wrong expiration date. My next stop would be a Bank of America branch. Just like the thieves, I'd present only my fake ID and my account number written on a blank slip from the lobby, and see if they'd let me withdraw money.

Whoops, slight problem. It's illegal to use fake ID in California, even if it's in your own name, even if you're taking out your own money. A lawyer I consulted told me I'd have to get a waiver from L.A. District

Attorney Steve Cooley to be a "confidential informant" about potential wrongdoing at the bank. But, before I could contact the DA, I got B of A's letter firing me as a customer, and it was all I could do to find a new bank and move my money before they threw it all out on the sidewalk, or whatever it is they do after dismissing you.

All along, I'd kept blogging about my experiences with B of A. After Consumerist.com[26] posted the e-mail address of B of A chair Kenneth Lewis, which I posted, dozens of my commenters copied me on e-mail they'd written him, telling him how horrified they were at the bank's "security" procedures and their treatment of me, and swearing they'd never bank there. Still, not everybody was buying into what I'd posted. One of the skeptics was "Jenn," the friend of one of my regular blog commenters, "Carrie."[27] Carrie left this comment on one of the B of A posts on my blog:

> I've been sharing this story with my friend Jenn who banks with BofA, much like Vlad she blamed the victim (Amy) and claimed her money was safe.
>
> We decided to test the system. Jenn gave me her account number and her drivers license. We look nothing alike. I've got about five inches and forty pound on Jenn; my hair is brown while she's a blond bomb shell with a nose out of this world.
>
> Like Amy, Jenn only makes infrequent ATM withdrawals for minimal amounts ($100 - $200).

---

26 One of my favorite blogs, with the motto "Shoppers Bite Back."

27 Not their real names!

Wednesday I was in another town for business and walked into a local BofA to see if I could withdraw money from Jenn's account, I told them "my" account number asked for $500 and handed them her license. A few taps latter I was told the available balance was $398 because it looked like my mortgage with country wide had just gone through and would I like to take the $398? I took $300 signed and walked out.

Needless to say, Jenn is closing her account as I type and moving to a local credit union. Here's the best part, as I'm standing waiting for the money my phone rings, I answer "This is Carrie" the bitch on the other side didn't even blink.

Wow. I needed to see if this would happen again. My boyfriend happened to be in Detroit, so I asked him to run a test for me—to go to a Bank of America teller window and try to withdraw money, replicating the actions of the thieves. I e-mailed him directions:

1. Use a withdrawal slip from the bank lobby and write your account number in.
2. Use only your driver's license to withdraw money. If they ask, and ONLY if they ask, you left your bank card in California.
3. Sign TOTALLY DIFFERENTLY from the way you usually sign.

He did this, and called me right after he left the bank—that same LaSalle Bank-turned-B of A near his mom's house (on East Warren Avenue). I couldn't believe what he told me, but here it is word for word:

I walked in the bank, filled out the withdrawal slip and I brought it over to a lady, and had my driver's license in my hand. I got up there and she goes, "Oh, out of state. Oh, we have a special form, another form." And she filled out something on the top, and then I filled in my name, my address as it appears on the license . . . city, date, zip, and then, telephone number.

So, I put in, kind of like, a couple of lazy digits. She asked me one point on my account number—she couldn't read the way I made a five—but you couldn't tell what the last few digits were on my phone. I signed it with the backward slant which made my signature somewhat different.

But this is the significant part: *I never had to show my driver's license, and I got the money.*

I had it [the license] in my hand. She saw it. It was there. At one point, I put it on the counter, and then I put it in my hand, fully expecting that she would ask me for my license. She dialed into the computer and it must've told her something.

Me: What, that your account had money in it?

Him: She just basically took my word for it, who I was.

95

This was stunning. Instead of verifying your ID when you go to withdraw money, does Bank of America simply HOPE it's you? Is it actually *impossible* for them, in many or all of their locations, to verify a customer's identity on their computers? The fact that the teller in the Midwest didn't even make *a show* of checking suggests that this is the case. A caveat: *Suggests.* I don't know this for sure. But, little or no verification of identity by B of A's tellers was a pattern that kept coming up. I had reason to believe I was on to something.

Then, one of my blog regulars pointed me to a Bank of America customer in Arizona named Chris Hooley. In a single day, in five separate transactions, Bank of America's tellers gave a thief $40,000 of his money. Hooley blogged it at chris-hooley.com:

> I saw the debit slip online, and this guy's signature wasn't even a remote attempt to copy mine. Okay, let's be fair: maybe they hired the blind. Maybe that particular teller was negligent. Or . . . could I really be right? I mean, how do you give out thousands of dollars without even verifying a signature?

Insane, huh? Bank of America is the largest commercial bank in America, yet you'd get more scrutiny trying to write a check for a bottle of Advil at the drugstore.

Bank of America wasn't always so big. They'd been on a long buying binge, gobbling up the credit card giant MBNA, then Countrywide Financial and Merrill Lynch, while continuing to buy and merge with numerous bank chains all over the damn place. In the wake of their mergers and acquisitions, especially in the past five years, I'd noticed a difference in the kind of employee they hired. It seemed they used to have grownups working there; for example, this very nice man, John Angello, who managed my branch. He not only went out of his way to do a good job for me and other customers I knew, he was the kind of guy you'd expect to run a bank. He looked like somebody's dad.

These days, employees at my now-former branch look like kids. Worse yet, they don't just *look* like kids. The day I'd learned of the thefts from my account, and I was in the branch at "Pauline's" desk waiting for her to get their fraud unit on the phone, an employee who looked about 18, but wore a button-down and a tie, was sitting at the desk behind me playing with a plastic slinky. Nonstop. For about 20 minutes. CH-CH-CH-CH-CH-CH! CH-CH-CH-CH-CH-CH! CH-CH-CH-CH-CH-CH!

At that point, I was terrified I might not get all my money back. So, there I was feeling totally at the bank's mercy, and this child in grownup's clothing, three feet behind me, was making this extremely annoying noise with his TOY! I wanted to say something, but I looked across the desk at Pauline at her computer, poring over the remains of my life savings, and I bit my tongue.

Reflecting later on Slinky Boy and other recent hires at my branch, I suspected they came cheap. I wondered whether customer privacy and security did, too. Is it possible that it's so costly to link all these newly acquired banks by computer, to the level they'd need to in order to verify signatures and other information, that Bank of America decided it's more profitable to just let customers take the hit?

If this is the case, it wouldn't be hard to imagine that thieves would learn about this, and B of A customers, especially, would be singled out for identity theft.

I started asking around about bank computer systems. A software engineer and commercial website developer who'd worked previously in banking e-mailed me this:

> Each bank as it grows uses independent computer systems that they purchase and use for a long, long time. When bank acquisitions are made then the acquired banks' different systems would need to be scrapped and replaced or there would need to be an adaptation made to sort of band-aid it into the new system. Developing and implementing new systems is incredibly costly.

It also takes time to wire two banks or a bunch of banks together. The software engineer said it isn't unreasonable for systems integration to take a year or two. The lawyer for the bank in the South told me that when her big bank merged with another big bank, their computer systems were integrated within 11 months. On the date the merger was official and the two banks became one, all bank employees were able to access all customer accounts "regardless of where they were." Likewise, in her previous job at a bank that used to buy a lot of smaller banks, "those banks would be connected to our computer systems on the official closing day of the merger."

Could it be possible that some banks, maybe even many banks, bought by Bank of America, *never* merged their computer systems?

What if Bank of America was actually many separate unconnected banks? The former LaSalle Bank my boyfriend went to was a recent B of A acquisition, but what about the computer systems at banks B of A had swallowed quite some time ago? Take First Gibraltar, a Texas bank acquired by Bank of America in 1993, turning my friend Kelly Boston, who banked at the Austin, Texas, First Gibraltar, into a B of A customer. Boston moved to Los Angeles over 10 years ago, in the mid-'90s, but left her account at the Austin B of A branch. To this day, at the B of A branch less than a mile from her house in Los Angeles, it's useless for her to swipe her bank card at the teller window because doing it won't pull up her account info.[28] "They sucked up my bank maybe 20 years ago," she said. "They never bothered to integrate everything. It probably costs too much money."

Boston once tried to transfer her account from Texas to the L.A. branch where she does all her banking. That would be impossible, B of A told her. She'd have to close her Texas B of A account and open a new account in Los Angeles. Mindful of not doing anything that would negatively affect her credit score, she asked how it would appear on her credit report. "They said it would show up as a totally new account," she said. They told her it was because the new account was in a new state, meaning, in her interpretation, "they were not connected . . . they were so disconnected that it was like being (with) a different bank."

---

28 My friend Virginia Postrel, who, like Kelly, made the move from Texas to L.A.—except for her still Texas-based B of A account—said she has the same experience at B of A teller windows in L.A. Other B of A customers confirm this.

At the end of July, there was one more bit of investigation I had to do while I was still a B of A customer. I called B of A's account services number and got chatty—my usual way of Hoovering information out of people. I talked to a rather on-the-ball girl I'll call Joanne. I told her that I'd felt I could trust B of A with my money, and then how shocked I was when they let my account be violated seven times, blah blah blah.

I mentioned my suspicions about the computers. Could it be possible that Bank of America just HOPES it's you? And "Joanne," bless her little heart, gave me what I needed, saying on July 26, 2008, around 8:45 A.M.:

"California accounts aren't in the database nationally."

Whoa.

I probed for more and she explained that B of A's banks don't all have access to the same database.

Double whoa.

Unless "Joanne" was wrong, it sounds like my suspicion is right—that once you go out of your metro area or maybe your state, Bank of America really does just *hope it's you*. Since tellers know they don't have the means to verify identity of out-of-state and maybe out-of-town customers (and perhaps even customers of different branches within a metro area), it's likely this information has not remained a secret from thieves.

It seems that B of A has put every one of their consumer banking customers in California, and perhaps the nation, at substantial risk for identity theft. Is it possible that *any* Bank of America customer could be victimized as I was, and that the only reason they haven't been is . . . *nobody's tried?*

I'm a fan of the late British economist Arthur Cecil Pigou's idea that the costs a business imposes on others should be factored into and paid from a business' profits. For a bank, it means not turning millions and millions of customers into attractive targets for identity theft by cheaping out on the computer systems necessary to protect them. At the very least, the bank should disclose the risk in banking with them—let customers and potential customers know when the reality of "multiple layers of security" simply means asking thieves, "Would you like our customer's money in tens, twenties, or hundreds?"

THE BUSINESS OF BEING RUDE, PART 2

Goofus and Gallant

"You're just a baby-sitter. You can't tell me what to do."

Gallant behaves when someone else is in charge.

Goofus gets a snack only for himself when friends are visiting.

Gallant asks permission to offer a snack to his friends.

SIDNEY QUINN

Courtesy of *Highlights for Children*

Gallant, Inc.

Let's be honest: Gallant, the good boy of *Highlights'* Goofus and Gallant duo, is kind of a bore—and that isn't such a bad thing. Bad boys do have their allure, even to girls who should know better, because they're exciting, unpredictable, challenging, and interesting—interesting along the lines of that Chinese curse, "May you live in interesting times."

This, however, is the story of a corporate good guy. It has its suspenseful moments, thanks to the perp, a guy who actually had no connection to the business where the crime occurred. But, because this particular company extended itself to protect the victim, this is a story that's kinda short on corporate intrigue.

In 2004, my column was finally in enough papers that my financial life wasn't a nonstop cliffhanger. I was driving an elegant junker, a $3,000 1970 Mercedes sedan that lacked airbags and farted out a lot of pollutants. I decided to buy my very first brand-new car—the hybrid Honda Insight, the most OPEC-starving, lung-friendly wheels I could find. Cute, too.

I loved my little car, and I soon learned to live with the lack of suspense that came with a new Honda, never again wondering as I got into the driver's seat whether my car would start, and if not, how much it would cost to make it. I was free to spend my money on new and exciting things, like exotic cheese. One Saturday in December, just before Christmas, I zipped over to the Wilshire Boulevard Whole Foods to see what they had.

Driving off the lot in September 2004 in my Honda.
Photo by Gregg Sutter.

I parked my car in their underground garage next to the grocery carts, went in and cheesed up. After I paid, I pushed my cart to my car. Just then, an old guy in a dark-colored car next to mine whipped out of his space—and when I say "whipped out," I mean like you would if you'd just robbed a bank. Weird. It's a grocery store parking garage, and a really P.C. granola grocery store at that. The guy sped out of the garage, and I stared after his car, some tricked-out older American number— what looked to be a designer edition Lincoln with a continental kit built right into the trunk. Because his behavior was so odd, I noted the license plate, one of the old blue and yellow ones, personalized with the word "EPICURE."

I just knew something was wrong. I examined my car. Sure enough, my almost brand-new Insight had a big gash in the rear fender panel, and the wheel skirt was no longer seated in place. Upon further examination, I found that the passenger door was closing funny. Great. Maybe there was frame damage.

I was really upset. When I got home, I called Whole Foods and asked the manager to review the video footage from their garage to see if "EPICURE" had indeed struck my car. He said somebody would, and told me to call back in a few days. When I did, he said "we" hadn't seen anything on the tape. Hmmm. Maybe because "we" hadn't actually looked? I asked to see it. The manager said it wasn't Whole Foods' policy to let me.

I called Whole Foods' corporate offices, and spoke with a customer relations person named Lourdes. She kept echoing what the store manager told me—no way could I see that tape. I made the argument that surely they have cameras in their garage to protect customers. I was a customer, and I wanted to be protected. I told her I would be out a bunch of money—at the very least my $500 deductible on my insurance—through no fault of my own, all because I had shopped at Whole Foods. Worse, there was some hit-and-run driver on the loose. I told her that I'd successfully tracked down a car thief in the past, and I wanted to use the tape to track this guy, build a case, and turn it over to the police so they could get him off the road.

Lourdes listened and told me she'd get back to me. Twenty minutes later, she did. (Yes, a mere 20 minutes—about as long as I'd once spent on hold with Bank of America, only to be informed nobody could help me.) Lourdes had good news—even better than I'd hoped for: Not only would I be allowed to see the tape, Whole Foods would burn me a copy. Woohoo!

The tape showed rows of parked cars in a parking garage. There was my little car. Vehicles came and went. A man on foot crossed the frame. And then, there it was: That weird old dark car lurched around the corner, stopped, backed up a little, and then made a wild arc into a parking space—slamming diagonally into the back right side of my car.

Unable to go forward, the driver backed up, straightened out his car, and pulled into the space. The driver's door opened, and an old man stepped out. He glanced at the damage he'd done to my car, looked around as if to see if anyone was looking, then walked off camera (toward the elevator up to the store). Yeah, that's right: He hit my car—so hard that the tape showed it rocking from the impact—and then went shopping! Unbelievable. From the wild way he swung into the space, and the fact that he had the audacity to do this hit-and-(somewhat-delayed)-run, I wondered whether he was tanked. I mean, if you're going to do a hit-and-run, do you go shop for gourmet chow between the hit and the run?

I took a copy of tape to the Santa Monica Police Department and made a police report. I learned that it would take some days for the report to be processed into their system and for an officer or detective to be assigned to the case—not that I was about to wait around for them to take action. After retrieving my own stolen pink Rambler, no thanks to the LAPD, I decided it was best to operate on the principle that the wheels of justice are likely to have one or more flat tires. And I'm not saying cops in general are negligent; maybe they're just busy solving murders or something.

My first step was finding out who the guy was. I did some research, and learned that I could request his car registration from the DMV. (They don't normally give this out, but they make an exception in a hit-and-run.) I filled out a DMV form and mailed it to Sacramento with a check for $5. Then, I took an educated guess as to where the guy lived and started driving around the neighborhood looking for his car in hopes of photographing paint scrapings from mine on his, along with any front-end damage. Since it was such an unusual-looking car, maybe somebody had seen it. I asked mail carriers, UPS drivers, unemployed actors, senior citizens on their daily walk. Nobody had any leads for me.

The car turned out to be registered to a woman—the wife of the creep who was driving. The DMV sent me her name, sans address, and a copy of her vehicle registration. The registration showed only dates from 1997 to 2004, with something interesting, "PRIOR SUSPENSE" in 1997. Interesting. I wondered what it was for. Unfortunately, as an ordinary citizen, I couldn't crack that info out of the DMV.

I Googled the woman like crazy and found out the name of her husband, Leo Laine (a.k.a. Lee Laine) apparently born in 1930, which made him 74 when he hit me. With his wife, he owned a Caribbean restaurant in the San Fernando Valley and opened another in West L.A. Before that, they'd owned a couple of Fatburger joints. A July 2004 *L.A. Daily News* review of the Laines' now-defunct Encino restaurant, Cha Cha Cha, called Laine "semi-retired." Yeah, right. Out of the restaurant business, into supermarket parking lot stock-car racing.

I called the police station every day to find out whether my case had been assigned. Two weeks later, it finally was. I was told to talk to an Officer H. I tried and tried—but he wouldn't call me back. Finally, I jogged to the police station. He came out into the lobby and I told him my story, and asked for EPICURE's insurance information so I could get my car fixed. Officer H. told me they "have procedure to follow": They first send a letter to the suspect asking whether he was involved in a hit-and-run. . .

Wait. A letter? I love it. Crime-stopping by pen pal. And what happens when the guy gets the letter, he just writes, "Nope, you must be mistaken!" and mails it back?[29]

As I'd expected, the police couldn't use the copy of the tape I'd made them (evidence rules—lest it'd been tampered with). Officer H. needed to get a copy directly from Whole Foods—just a mile or two from the police station. I called every few days to ask whether he'd gotten it. Finally, almost a month after I made the police report, he did. Well? He said he'd brought Laine in to view the tape.

"What?" I couldn't help myself. "You don't show the guy the evidence!" I exclaimed.

He got angry. "Don't tell me how to do my job!"

I apologized—and I was sincerely sorry, mainly that I'd scored him as the cop on my case.

He then told me, "Even after viewing the videotape, he's not admitting or denying that he hit your car."

And? And that's that? He told me it was the city attorney's decision whether to take the case any further. Maybe that would happen, maybe not. None-too-pleased, I took Laine's insurance information from Officer H. and called the company, Mercury Insurance. They

---

29 The LAPD employed a similar approach after the phone company traced an obscene caller who'd been harassing me in the wee hours. The detective said the guy, who'd made the calls from his cell, told her "a friend" "might've" had his phone. "At 3:00 A.M., month after month after month?" I asked her. She told me he'd promised to call her back with that person's information. What a shocker, he never did.

denied my claim. I spent about two hours fighting with their agent on the phone and she resubmitted it. On February 4, they sent me a letter calling their investigation "incomplete," and encouraged me to make a claim with my own insurance company—meaning I'd be paying my $500 deductible and maybe end up seeing an increase in my insurance premium. Nuh-uh. No way. I refused to let up, and they finally made arrangements to fix my car. With some wrangling, I even got them to rent me a hybrid while mine was in the shop. (Why should I pollute the air unnecessarily just because some jerk they were unwise enough to insure did a number on my car?)

I was still disturbed by Officer H.'s intimation that it was sort of iffy as to whether the guy would be prosecuted. Silly me, thinking all I had to do was track down a hit-and-run driver, present the police with a neat package of evidence, and the guy would be brought to justice. A lawyer-friend gave me the name of one of the deputy city attorneys, Marsha Moutrie, and told me to write up the case, send it to her, and ask her to have her office prosecute the guy. And so I wrote. And so they prosecuted.

On May 15, 2005, in "Airport Court," the new criminal court near LAX, Leo Laine stood before Judge Bernard Kamins and pled no lo contendere[30] to a misdemeanor hit-and-run. (Had I been injured, he would've been charged with a felony.) Judge Kamins placed Laine on 24 months' probation and fined him $717 plus "restitution" (the cost, paid by his insurance company, of fixing my car). Laine also did

---

30 Neither admitting nor denying guilt—a tactic sometimes used to avoid having criminal judgments used in civil cases.

one day of jail time. Amazingly, the guy seemed remorseless, glowering at me in court. Hey, old man, I didn't hit *your* car.

A couple months later, I called Laine and told him I was planning to sue him in Santa Monica Small Claims Court for $5,000 for the time his hit-and-run cost me. (This is actually the first step this court has you take in suing somebody—asking to be paid the money.) I factored in every bit of my time (63 hours and 15 minutes according to my log), for everything from my own detective work to arguing with his insurance company, to getting my car fixed to spending an afternoon in court, and added in my out-of-pocket costs for parking, DVDs, and records requests from the cops and the DMV. I offered to settle for $2,000. Laine refused. Ever remorseless, he snapped, "We're going to sue you!"

"Um, why?" (This had to be good.)

"We're going to sue you for suing us!"

I had to laugh. I actually wasn't about to put time and energy into dragging him back to court—I just thought I'd try, the easy way, to get him to pay me, since he really did owe me for the time I'd spent. Also, I thought it was good to at least make the guy believe his actions might lead to another unpleasant day in the judicial system, and another sock in the wallet.

Finally, from the way I saw the guy driving on the tape, I suspected he was somebody who shouldn't be behind the wheel. I wrote to his son, a doctor and a university professor:

A suggestion: I know it's hard to think of a parent perhaps becoming infirm, but to avoid tragedies like the one at the

Santa Monica farmers' market,[31] I strongly urge you to get his vision and ability to drive checked out. We had to take the tough step to take my grandpa's keys away, but it was the right thing to do. Perhaps, in this case, it is as well.

Big difference, huh, in the stories of Goofus, Inc., and Gallant, Inc., a.k.a. Bank of America and Whole Foods?

Bank of America was spectacularly negligent, never doing the most minimum due diligence to verify identity. All they had to do was check a signature just one of those seven times. They have armed guards in the bank; they could've held the thief for the police, and that fake license in my name would surely be in a police evidence locker right now. And maybe, just maybe, those two women would've named names, perhaps of some identity theft ring, and perhaps pointed the way to B of A insiders selling customer information. And maybe, just maybe, that would keep a lot of other B of A customers from having months or years of their lives eaten by the perpetual hell that is identity theft.

Most disgustingly, Claudius and other enablers at the bank portrayed the violations of my account as something that *just happened*—as unexpectedly and unconnected to any action or inaction by the bank as a meteorite falling out of the sky. Never admitting their wrongdoing meant never taking responsibility for it, never liv-

---

31 In 2003, an 86-year-old retired salesman named George Weller put his foot on the gas instead of the brake in his Buick, and careened through the Santa Monica farmer's market, killing 10 people and injuring many others.

ing up to the old kindergarten standard, "Clean up your own mess." Even worse, when I begged them to allow me to clean up their mess by giving me the video footage I needed to protect myself and maybe others—they refused.

Meanwhile, Whole Foods, merely the staging area for a hit-and-run, handed over the videotape after just a bit of wrangling by me. Then, there's the fact that they have video cameras in their garage and probably for the reason I suspect—to protect their customers. And because they extended themselves on behalf of this customer, I did what I'd originally intended to in the B of A case: I focused my attention entirely on tracking down the perp; I didn't, say, start making trips out to organic farms to see exactly how happy the chickens are.

Thanks to Bank of America's aggressive refusal to behave accountably and give me the videotape they owed me by law, all I could do was hone in on them and their reprehensible business practices (I'm continuing to try to expose them in the media and through government watchdogs as this book goes to press). And while there are still two thieves running around with a fake license in my name (maybe one of whom has by now used my money to get teeth), being denied the evidence I needed to track them ended up being something of a good thing. After all, in the end, Bank of America turned out to be a far bigger perp than the two women who stole my money.

THE UNDERPARENTED CHILD

The thing that impresses me the most about America is the way parents obey their children.

—England's King Edward VIII (1894–1972)

The guy above wasn't even talking about parents today. He died in '72, when I was eight. Back then, I believed I could fly, but the idea that I could ever be loud in a restaurant or kick the back of somebody's seat in a movie theater did not exist for me in what was possible in the known universe. I credit my parents, who I sometimes describe as "loving fascists." Our roles were clear. They were the parents and I was the child. They gave the orders and I obeyed them. ("Heil, Mother!")[32]

---

32 My book editor, who, unlike me, errs on the side of good taste, wanted me to cut this. As a godless harlot who grew up Jewish, I'm invoking my right to make un-PC Nazi jokes.

These days, too, American familial roles are clear. There are kings and queens and there are lowly serfs—serfs called parents whose single greatest fear is not being liked by their children. As a result, as I wrote in a column, "The parental 'no' has officially joined the ranks of chronically missing items like The Holy Grail, Atlantis, and Britney Spears' underpants."

I was responding to an e-mail from a mother wracked with guilt because she longed for a break from accommodating her kids' requests "for food, more food, different food, a checkers partner, a Lego partner, and someone to read 'Hand, Hand, Fingers, Thumb' for the 40th time since breakfast." Like so many parents these days, she had her role all wrong, I told her:

> You're supposed to be your kids' mom, not their full-time birthday clown. This means meeting their needs, as opposed to falling prey to their ransom demands; i.e., "Send in the cupcakes or I'll scream my lungs out until spring!"
>
> If you're keeling over from reading "Hand, Hand, Fingers, Thumb" 40 times, it's because you didn't say no 39 times. "No" is also the correct response when besieged with requests for a chunky peanut butter sandwich with all the chunkies removed. But, children can be such finicky eaters! Correction: American children can be such finicky eaters, because their parents tend to confuse parenting with working room service at a five-star hotel. In France, on the other hand, the kids' meal is whatever the parents are eating; brains, livers, kidneys and all. And while the kids can pick out bits they don't like, their choice is clear: eat or starve.

Saying no to your kids will not turn them into meth-smoking, liquor store-robbing carjackers. Actually, throwing up a few boundaries might even serve to prevent this—and less dire but extremely annoying outcomes (just what society needs, another 35-year-old snot who was denied nothing during childhood).

Of course, these days, the mere suggestion of imposing restrictions on children sends parents on the warpath. A reader of my column who signed herself "Mother Of The Bride-To-Be" learned this the hard way when planning her daughter's wedding, "a formal evening reception featuring champagne and dancing" (and no, that isn't code for "a playground-side event catered by Ronald McDonald, featuring Super Soak The Groom and Pin-The-Tail-On-The-Bride"). Accordingly, they printed "Adult Reception" on the invitation—as opposed to the more straightforward "Leave the loud, underparented brats at home."

"You cannot imagine the trauma this has caused," wrote the woman. Parents were furious, deeply offended that their children weren't welcome. "We don't have the budget to have lots of children at the reception," the woman explained. "But, more importantly, my daughter, her fiancé, and I feel a formal evening event is not appropriate for children. Were we out of line, and do we need to apologize?"

Apologize? Well, you could—with something along the lines of "Excuse me if I'd rather not have Daddy's toast to his daughter's happiness interrupted by some giant, still-breastfeeding five-year-old screaming, 'I WANT BOOBY!'" I, in turn, expressed my own regret—that there are too few out there like Mother Of The Bride-To-Be. As for parents who get indignant at the need to hire a sitter, if this was going to be an issue, well, they should've used protection.

In case it isn't apparent, this chapter isn't about bad children, it's about bad parents. The children, like cell phones in the hands of loud narcissists, are merely a medium through which self-involved so-called adults inflict themselves on the rest of us. Unfortunately, while you need a license to cut hair, you need only working ovaries to have a child.

In 1965, Jack Weinberg, the leader of the Free Speech Movement, made a crack to a *San Francisco Chronicle* reporter, "We have a saying in the movement that we don't trust anybody over 30." He later told *The Washington Post* that he didn't actually believe that; it was meant as a kind of taunt.[33] But, that sort of thinking caught on, and it eventually started to be uncool, not only to trust anyone over 30, but to be over 30.

In *The Weekly Standard*, contributing editor Joseph Epstein traced the decline of parenting back to the late '60s and early '70s when adulthood went out of vogue, starting with clothes and extending to personal conduct. Kids on the cusp of adulthood revolted against the conventional, the lives of their parents, by refusing to become them. Essentially, they refused to grow up. But, it wasn't just a teen rebellion phase. As Epstein writes, "Everyone, even people with children and other adult responsibilities, wanted to continue to think of himself as young, often well into his 40s and 50s."

---

33 Bartleby.com.

I actually love the blurring of the adult-child line, the way most of my friends act mostly like adults—working, paying taxes, not hitting others over the head with a plastic shovel when they don't get their way—yet they also seem perpetually young and cool. The problem comes when a parent's need to remain young and cool takes precedence over assuming what Epstein calls "the old parental role of authority figure, dealing out rewards and punishments and passing on knowledge." Starting in the late '60s, Epstein writes, "parents wanted their children to think of them as, if not exactly contemporaries, then as friends, pals, fun people."

A few decades later, the adult-child line is no longer blurred; it's snarled. We've got eight-year-old girls dressing like hookers while their mothers dress like eight-year-old girls. Last week, I stood in line behind a big white vinyl Hello Kitty purse—on the arm of a 40-something mother of two. Forty-something dads bicker with their kids over whose turn it is on the Nintendo, and sociologist Frank Furedi wrote on Spiked.com about trying to wean his two-year-old son off "Teletubbies," and realizing the futility of it after spotting a bunch of undergraduates glued to an episode of the show in a bar.

Welcome to Never Never Land! The grownup boyfriend of a grownup friend pulls her bubble-gum pink Hello Kitty suitcase through Paris. (If that's not love, what is?) *Photo by Jackie Danicki*

Your World Is Their Day-Care Center

There used to be kid spaces and adult spaces. In fact, I thought kids and I had a deal: I'd stay out of Chuck E. Cheese if they stayed out of the martini lounge. Nope. In New York and some other places, kids can go to bars, and do. You amble into the local gin joint and, for a moment, you're not quite sure whether you've entered an adult drinking establishment or a nursery school parking lot, what with all the Cadillac Escalade-sized strollers crowding the place.

Bar talk just isn't the same. Mommies tossing 'em back loudly debate the merits of various breast pumps. Embarrassed regulars get told "Okay, Mister, so look the other way when the lady's breastfeeding!" And hey, "Watch your language, sailor! There are children present!" Of course, even with kids in the tavern, there are still bar fights. It's the topics that've changed: "Anson took my truck!" "Did not!" "Did too!"

If you're a bar owner, don't even dream of telling parents they can't turn your place into Romper Room With Beer. That's what the owners of Brooklyn's Union Hall dared to do, with two signs, "Please, No Strollers" and "No One Under 21 Admitted." Their bar, their rules, right? Wrong. Shortly afterward, the mommies in the neighborhood declared war. "Local parenting blogs were soon bristling with denunciations," reported Alex Williams in *The New York Times*.

"This was a perfect winter moms' group place for those of us with infants going stir-crazy," wrote one woman on onlytheblogknowsbrooklyn.com, wondering testily why local mothers could not at least drop in for "a beer once a week when it's not crowded."

Um, because it's a *bar*, lady. Take it from another parent, commenting below Williams' story:

> I have a six year old and a three year old. I like
> going out as much as the next person. Still, there
> are places that are appropriate for children, and
> places that are not. If it's not a place where the
> management and clientele can handle spilled juice,
> random Cheerios, and children underfoot, then don't
> go. It's not fair to the kids or to other patrons.

Delving into the motivation of those determined to inflict their children on bar patrons, Williams quoted writer/actress Christen Clifford, who, most charmingly, sees dragging her baby to the martini lounge as a way of denying that one's youthful exploits come with a shelf life. "Psychologically, you feel like, 'Oh, my life hasn't changed that much,'" she said, "although of course it completely has."

Okay, fine, a mommy likes to dream, but why should that mean the adult social scene of the rest of us gets turned into a playdate? Guess what, lady: The feminists were wrong. Sadly, tragically, you cannot "have it all"—not when it means making the rest of us put up with it all. So, if you're a parent, and you simply must throw back a beer or two while minding the kiddies, please feel free to pop into the liquor store for a six-pack on your way home.

Meanwhile, you might ask yourself, how good can it be for the kiddies to be doing all this grownup stuff when they're still a decade or decades away from actual grownuphood? Even age-old bastions of adulthood, like the Manhattan culinary landmark and power broker dining spot The Four Seasons, are opening their doors to the stroller set, offering a "Children's Day." Childfree bloggers "Josie Hawk" and "Ruby Stoneheart" (TakeBackTheIsland.wordpress.com) were aghast:

> Can't there be any things that are reserved just for grownups? Kids don't need fucking "mommy and me" spa treatments or virgin cocktails. When I was a little kid I watched my mom get ready to go out somewhere fancy with my dad and dreamed about getting to do the same thing one day. . . . You can give your precious snowflake an expensive meal, but she still might throw a tantrum at dinner or say that the foie gras is gross. It's OK to make shit not be kid friendly.

I can choose to leave a bar any time I find the clientele not to my liking. Bailing is more difficult in other places I encounter little devilspawn, like while hurtling through the air in a cramped steel tube.

Asking parents on a plane or anywhere else to actually parent their wee savages is usually futile. If they were inclined to parent in the first place, there'd be no need for you to make the request. Knowing this, I sometimes make my appeal right to the source, like I did on a long flight when a boy, about nine, playing his Gameboy or something, kept hollering out his own name—"Yah, Hunter!"—every time he scored.[34] I assumed this kid was being sent across the

---

34 My friend Cathy Seipp commented, "Do you think Hunter will be shouting 'Way to go, Hunter!' when he grows up and starts having sex?"

country on a plane by himself. I assumed wrong. The kid was seated with his mother and father, neither of whom thought to instruct him to put himself on mute.

The little old lady next to me asked me to help her work the movie contraption at her seat. I started pulling up choices on the remote. "Classic or new releases?" I asked her. She couldn't hear me. Neither, in fact, could I. I turned to the shouting boy, whose mother had disappeared, probably to the restroom. My impulse was to snarl at him, *Exorcist* style, "Shut up, you underparented cur!" Instead, I opted for a tone a little more Bambi, and pleaded, "Could you please keep it down a bit? It's very distracting."

I went back to helping the old lady. Thirty seconds later, the kid was hollering again—this time, at a boy who'd taken his mother's seat next to him. (The mother was still nowhere to be seen.) I shot a purposeful look to the kid's father, put my finger to my lips and made a "Shhhh" sound. Now Dad could take charge. Dad? Dad? It seems Dad found *Newsweek* extremely compelling.

I finally got *Cold Mountain* to play for the little old lady. Just then, Mom came back. Apparently, Hunter informed her that I'd asked him to cut the shouting. Mom was outraged. She glared at me. "What did you say to my son?!" Almost speechless, I stammered, "Well . . . your child was shouting, and it's disturbing, because we're *(look around you, assbrain!)* in rather close quarters!"

Was she horrified? She was indeed. By me. She turned to her Precious, and, caressing his cheek, cooed, "Don't listen to her, Hunter, don't you listen to her." *Caressing his cheek!*

I do take precautionary measures whenever I fly—noise-canceling headphones and Hearos earplugs *(Hearos Xtreme Super Soft Foam ear filters, with the highest noise reduction, NRR 33)*. I don't expect absolute quiet from kids or anyone; I just expect parents to expect their kids to be considerate of others, and to intervene when they're not. On a positive note, when I see well-behaved children on a plane or elsewhere, I compliment and thank the parents; usually while digging in my handbag for a bath towel to mop up my tears of gratitude.

Should airplanes have a section of the plane reserved for parents with babies and younger children? When airfarewatchdog.com asked that question, 58 percent of the 20,116 people who responded voted for an airplane kiddie ghetto, clicking "Yes, they should have done this long ago." Another 27 percent were also in favor of airlines establishing it, but clicked "Yes, but they never will and it'll never work." Only 15 percent (2,974 people) clicked "No. This is a bad idea."

My take on it? Yes, they should have done this long ago, and no, they never will (since even parents with screaming children don't want to sit near parents with screaming children). Except in cases of emergency where a parent can't help but travel with their little howler monkey, my suggestion is that parents themselves set up a special seating area for their children still in the feral stage—in the parents' own living room.

If the kiddies must see Granny, and Granny lives a plane flight away and is well enough to travel, why not send the old girl a plane ticket? Like many children, she may require "special assistance" in boarding, but she probably won't spend the flight like a kid behind me did for much of the 14 hours from Paris back to Los Angeles:

banging a plastic cup on his tray table and punching and kicking my seat like he was training for his first prize-fight. For the record, his parents thought I was a real witch for asking them to make him stop. "He's just a boy!" the father said at one point, as if that made it all okay.

Thankfully, there are some parents who think to edit themselves out of the public sphere until their children are domesticated. My friend Hillary Johnson was one of them, showing exemplary consideration for beleaguered busboys and the eardrums of the rest of us:

> When my son Tyrone was about a year old, my ex and I found ourselves in one of those binds—we really needed to just go to a restaurant (tired, cranky), but we had an equally tired, cranky one-year-old. Our solution? The coffee shop at the bowling alley! Surely we would be within the polite decibel range in such environs . . .well, we were, until Tyro braced his pudgy little legs against the lip of the formica table and kicked it over, spraying icewater and french fries in a 20 foot radius. That was our last restaurant visit for several years. I simply arranged my life otherwise for that period of time. I found that staying home was a great way to avoid stress—for me and the other 10 million inhabitants of L.A.

Eventually, parents do have to unlock the tower room and let the kids out into the world. My neighbors help their four-year-old girl and eight-year-old boy learn restaurant etiquette by taking them out to eat at the times and places they're least likely to bother other patrons: around 6 P.M. at family restaurants where there's such a din that the occasional "BUT I WANT MACARONI!" blends right in. And yes, kids will be kids. But, when these kids act up, their dad is quick to take them outside, not only showing consideration for others but teaching his kids the importance of it.

When friends and acquaintances who've read my blog items on The Underparented Child hear how fondly I speak of my neighbors' kids, they're sometimes surprised; as in, how did a child-loathing meanie like me end up such a puddle of adoration for these two children—to the point where I really miss them when their mother takes them camping for a day or two? It really hasn't taken a lot to get me to this point, and that isn't because my neighbors have the world's first Stepford children.

Their kids do, on occasion, wake me up seriously early on a Sunday morning, and the little boy is always inventing some new game that involves repeatedly banging some hard object on the paved walk between our houses when I'm trying to write. For me, what makes all the difference is hearing their parents say, "Shhh, come over and play in our yard, Amy might be sleeping." The fact that they care makes me respond to the BANG! BANG! BANG!-ing with a head-shake and a laugh, then open a window and remind the little boy that I'm an old bag who needs her beauty sleep.

Also, my neighbors never sneer what underparenters in public places sometimes do when I ask them to contain their children— "Are YOOOOOU a parent?!"—as if only those who have spawned are qualified to have or express an opinion on the public behavior of somebody's little wildlings. I don't have or want kids; in fact, I sometimes describe myself as "BARREN!" And while I've actually read piles of research on raising and educating kids, and attended psych conference presentations on the subject by luminaries like John Gottman and Peter Gray, the how-to of teaching kids manners and setting boundaries for them is not some rare and inaccessible form of mysticism. Of course, merely squeezing out a child doesn't turn a person into a child psychology expert, but "Are YOOOOOU a parent?!" is a trick question, meant to deflect attention from the shriekingly obvious: someone's flagrant failure to actually parent.

If, like me, you have yet to reproduce, be prepared for parents to use this question as a weapon if you try to set even the most minimum standards for children's conduct in public. In a *New York Times* piece on rowdy children in coffee shops, Jodi Wilgoren reported that Dan McCauley, a Chicago café owner, dared post the sign, "children of all ages have to behave and use their indoor voices when coming to A Taste of Heaven." Mothers were outraged. "I love people who don't have children who tell you how to parent," Alison Miller, a 35-year-old psychologist, corporate coach, and mother of two, complained. "I'd love for him to be responsible for three children for the next year and see if he can control the volume of their voices every minute of the day."

Okay, I get that it's difficult. But the truth is, Alison, the rest of us don't want to tell you how to parent. We just want you to do it. There's playground behavior and there's restaurant behavior. We don't want our dining interrupted by your screaming kids because you haven't considered whether they are (1) clear on the difference, and (2) mature enough to handle sitting through an entire meal. Should your child begin jumping up and down on his chair, we'd like you to stop him, then wipe the seat. If he has a meltdown, don't just hope it will pass. Maybe even interrupt your conversation with your friend and take the kid outside. When you do, I'm not going to storm out after you and lecture you on your parenting. I'll probably just sit there feeling a little wellspring of compassion for you rising up in my little black coal lump of a childless heart. Again, it really is that simple. You just have to show you care.

Granted, not all kids are so responsive to commands—and it helps to know when the reason for that isn't lax parenting. My friend Heather spent a few years annoyed at the mother of a boy in her daughter's school who always seemed out of control. When Heather's toddler son was diagnosed with autism, Heather mentioned it to the woman. The woman confessed, "My son has autism, too." Suddenly, the kid's behavior made sense. "You should've said something!" Heather told her. Instead, the woman had hidden it, perhaps out of embarrassment, perhaps thinking it would help the kid "pass."

Heather takes the absolute opposite approach. She brings her son to select public engagements like her daughter's elementary school dance recital so he can learn how to act in public. When she does, she'll tap people around her on the shoulder and ask them to spread the word: "I just want to warn you ahead of time, my son has autism, and he may burst out in excitement, and I apologize for any discomfort it might cause." The response is always "Oh, no, not a problem," Heather said. But, not only do people appreciate the heads-up, Heather finds that they seem to welcome the opportunity to extend a little generosity of spirit. I'm not surprised. People, even cranky childless people like me, will give a kid a break if you just clue them in.

Cutting "special needs" kids some slack is one thing. I draw the line at accommodating special needs parents—parents who seem convinced they're very, very special by virtue of having reproduced, and need to make the rest of us understand that by showing us exactly how little we matter.

Two of these special needs parents, both mommies, dropped in one morning at the Rose Café, perhaps hoping to enhance the ambience by punctuating the classical music, clinking glasses, and the dull murmur of adult conversation with the uninterrupted shrieks of their babies. The pained faces around me told me I wasn't the only one who was bothered, so I went over to the mommies and, failing to be mindful of their status as reproductive royals and mine as a childless commoner, suggested they "could be a little more considerate." And yes, they could—but, of course they wouldn't, and how dare I even suggest such a thing? One mother gave me the finger repeatedly, and asked, "What do lonely, angry bitches like you know?" She did eventually propose a solution: that I look in the mirror at my "ugly face"—as if this would help me put a cork in her kid. I had a different solution in mind, a bit of blogslapping. Smile big for the camera, ladies!

In the *LA Weekly*, I wrote about another mother I encountered at the Rose—one who seemed utterly unwilling to modify her choice of lunch spot, even if it meant gambling that her two small children wouldn't end up broken on the hard linoleum floor like two little Humpty Dumpties. This well-heeled pregnant mommy plopped her sobbing toddler down at a tall table on a very toddler-unsafe-looking tall stool, and her other kid, a boy around four, on another, and walked away to stand in the long line for food and coffee. When she did, the toddler started kicking the steel leg of the chair and intermittently yelling and howling.

This went on for quite some time. I had a choice: suffer in silence or say something. I caught the toddler's eye. "You need to be quiet," I told him, softly but firmly. "It makes it not nice for all the other people here if you're making all this noise, so please stop right now." And miracle of miracles, that was all it took to make him button his tiny yap and stop kicking the chair: a lone adult voice from beyond that vast sea of "go-right-ahead" mommying, telling him, firmly, but not cruelly, that his howling would not be tolerated.

Neither, for that matter, would my intervention. His mother marched over to my table, shaking with rage, and demanded, "Did you just reprimand my child?!" I told her I did. Her jaw dropped—all the way to the stretchy stomach of her chic LA yoga-mommy maternity wear. "It isn't your job to reprimand my child!"

BAD SANTA

A friend of mine—passive-aggressive because aggressive-aggressive takes so much work—likes to use birthdays and holidays to "give back" to underparenters in her family and social circle. She looks for just the right craft sets; for example, thousand-piece bead kits with those all-important two words on the package: "loose glitter." She also favors drum sets, kazoos, karaoke machines, talking Teletubbies, and the *Dora the Explorer Choo Choo* talking book. Yes, little Madison will just find joy in making Dora make that choo-choo sound hundreds of times a day! (Don't forget to ask for the address of her mommy's sanitarium so you can send flowers.)

I agreed with her—no, it isn't my job—and what a shame that the person whose job it *is* isn't doing it, leaving the task to irritable strangers in cafés.

When In America, Do As The French Do

Now, I'm not one of those who looks down on everything American and thinks everything French is *la bombe*. But, for over a decade, I've been going to Paris several times a year, often for a month at a time, so I've got more than a tourist's take on French culture, the good and the bad. My friend M., a Paris-dwelling American married to a French woman, jokes that the French are great at three things, "The Three 'Fs,'" he calls them: Food, Fashion, and, uh, l'Amour. Actually, make that four things: They also know a thing or two about raising kids.

In France, you rarely hear a child screeching in a public place, and certainly not for any length of time. If a child does get even the slightest bit out of hand, total strangers, especially elderly people, will feel quite free to correct him. In response, the child's parent or parents (who will likely be mortified at the need) will not scream, dial the French version of 911, or chew the reprimander out. In fact, they might even thank the person.

Author Janine di Giovanni wrote in the British paper *The Telegraph* of a Parisian friend who took her five-year-old son to the park and had to tell him repeatedly not to do something. An elderly woman suddenly reached over and pinched her son's ear until he squealed. "Listen to your mother," she said sternly.

Di Giovanni's friend, born American but raised in Paris, wasn't offended. She explained that she understood that the old lady, "and every other French grandmother," would think it's for the good of the child. "Anglo-Saxons tend to see children as charmingly thick savages who can be taught manners in a superficial way. The French grasp the deeper meaning of civilised behaviour as soon as they can speak, and drill it into them."

My bicontinental friend Debra Ollivier, author of books like *What French Women Know*, explaining the French to us Anglos, told me about a meeting with the director of a school in Paris when she was looking to enroll her five-year-old son. After the interview, the lady went to shake her son's hand. He held out his left, and the director "stood up straight and in an almost punitive tone, said 'Mais non! Do not shake with your left hand. Please shake with your right hand!'"

Ollivier said, "The American part of me thought she was being an uptight French poodle, but the French part of me appreciated the feedback from someone in a position of authority; that's how kids learn, not just from their parents but from authority figures and people outside the family."

Of course, it helps that French families still maintain traditional parent-child roles—the kind we used to have in America. Cross-cultural business consultants Gilles Asselin and Ruth Mastron, in their book, *Au Contraire! Figuring Out The French*, allude to these roles in explaining why French children are not allowed to interrupt adult conversations the way American children do. "French adults generally consider that the child's interests and needs in most cases should not supersede adult concerns, and accordingly, teach the child to understand and accept limitations" on his actions and expression. This, they write, helps children learn proper manners and behavior, which the French see as essential to their success in school and in adult life.

Because French parents see it as normal—even important, as a learning experience—for their children to fall down and get hurt, there is one place French children have a level of free reign that many overprotected American kids do not: on the playground. At home, however, the rules are numerous and strict. French children are not only expected to eat whatever is being served at the dinner table, meals are eaten with the whole family, and children are not allowed to pop up from the table until the parents excuse them at the end of the meal. From age two, they are drilled in proper table manners, which include correct use of utensils and the appropriate tone of voice. Essentially, they're treated like shorter adults.

Accordingly, my friend Emmanuelle Richard, a French journalist and mother living in Washington, D.C., said it's "super-hard" to find restaurants in France with high chairs and other paraphernalia specifically for children because, if kids come in, they are expected to "behave like adults and blend in." Should you see a young child out in a Paris restaurant with his parents and grandparents on some special occasion, chances are, he will not only be sitting still and upright in his chair, he'll have table manners to rival those of Jackie O.

While American parents allow their children to dominate conversation, encouraging them to yammer on as if their every word is a little gold nugget coming into existence, French children are expected to learn conversational restraint. Should a French child start babbling at the family dinner table, another cultural exchange expert, Polly Platt, author of *French or Foe?* reports that the parental reply is often "That's boring," or "You're just trying to get attention," in order to train the child to wait to speak until he has something witty or worthwhile to say. That will surely seem cruel and maybe even incomprehensible to a lot of Americans, but remember the goal: They're trying to prepare their children for the real world. That's exactly the opposite of what so many Americans have begun to do, like with the way at least one local Little League has become Little Coddled League.

Comedian Jay Mohr wrote in *Sports Illustrated* about accompanying his godson to his ballgame. After the kid hit what looked like a homer, he inexplicably stopped running at second base, and just stood there waiting while the other team chased down the ball. Mohr, confused, turned to a friend, and the guy explained—this particular league *doesn't allow* home runs: "Parents don't like it when their children are made to feel bad by being crushed by a home run, so all home runs in this league are only doubles."

"WHAT!!! Are you kidding me?" Mohr couldn't believe it. "Do you want to know who I feel bad for? The mini man standing on second base who was denied the glorious feeling of hitting his first bomb." Mohr then went French on the coddlers: "Why not teach kids at a young, impressionable age that there are winners and losers? Sometimes you win, sometimes you lose. That's what the game—and life—is all about."

It Wasn't Mousse au Chocolat

Like bird flu, narcissism knows no boundaries. While the French are practically imprinted down to the chromosome with an entire encyclopedia of public protocol, an individual Frenchwoman can know the exact correct behavior in a situation and still not let herself be inconvenienced by it.

A few months after I was horrified by a woman changing her baby's diaper at her table at my local hippie haus of coffee, I was in Paris with my boyfriend, having coffee and pastry with two Parisian friends at chi-chi Ladurée (the Tiffany's of pâtisseries). At a big round table in the middle of the dining room—effectively center stage—a woman who looked to be a posh Parisian mommy laid her baby right on the table, undid the kid's poopy diaper, and began wiping the kid's butt! As I wrote on my blog:

> I'll say this in as colorfree a way as I can: the *contents of the diaper* were completely visible to me and probably to most of the patrons. The woman took her sweet time, too, placidly going through the whole diaper-changing process right then and there on the table—despite the fact that she was a mere 10 feet from a very nice restroom with a rather ample marble sink/vanity area. I'm getting sick all over again just writing about it.

In France, the kingdom of rules and the high church of food, you may find it impossible to get a coffee served with your salad ("Madame, le café is for after the meal," the waiter will lecture you)—but this woman's behavior was so beyond the pale, nobody knew what to do. Restaurant staff stood frozen, mouths agape. The four of us went momentarily mute. I was seated a little further away than my boyfriend, so I handed him my camera and asked him to take a photo.

Changing her baby in the middle of Ladurée pâtisserie, Paris. *Photo by Gregg Sutter*

The woman finally finished her baby-changing, and they left. Busboys sped over and stripped the table bare and carted off everything on it. I wouldn't be surprised if they'd burned the thing afterward.

Now, this little incident happened back in 2005, before there were a whole lot of Paris bloggers, Anglo or French, so my posting never led to the identification and public embarrassment of the guilty that I'd hoped for. But, should you ever see this sort of thing, in America or across the pond, one of my blog commenters, a woman who lives in France, had a suggestion:

> Amy, the only thing wrong with the photograph is that Gregg took it from his seat instead of doing a close up. Had I been in that situation, I would have got up & taken the picture right in front of the baby's ass, *caca* included. Maybe this inconsiderate couple would have got the message.

Goodnight Already, Moon!

Other than posting the occasional blogslapping of those who have weaponized their children and set them loose on the rest of us, I'm actually not that motivated to seek revenge against parents. I don't have to. I take solace in the idea that the results of their underparenting will soon come home to roost—that is, if they ever left.

Think it's the rare 35-year-old who's still sleeping in his childhood bunk bed? That's not what a slew of books suggests—titles like *101 Ways to Get Your Adult Children to Move Out (And Make Them Think It Was Their Idea)* and *Boomerang Nation: How to Survive Living with Your Parents . . . the Second Time Around.* I just loved *Boomerang Nation*'s very first paragraph:

> Good news! Most people moving home today will find that the stigma of living at home has all but disappeared. Having come out of the basement, boomerangers are loud, proud, and not afraid to show the world that they mean business. With so many boomerangers returning to the nest around the world, it's become clear that we boomerangers are not going away anytime soon.

Yes, while you and I might suffer the immediate results of underparenting, the perpetrators will have a lifetime to experience the joy that coddled children, unprepared to pay rent, utilities, or hold down a job, can provide. I can just hear it now, that adult male voice calling down from upstairs: "Hey, Ma! Another beer!"

8

IT'S ONLY FREE FOR TELEMARKETERS TO CALL YOU BECAUSE YOU HAVE YET TO INVOICE THEM

There are a number of reasons I have a telephone: to talk to my friends and family, to suck up to editors, to call my landlord at 3 A.M. when the roof's leaking and it's raining on my pillow, and to ring the fire department if I smell smoke. Note the conspicuous absence on this list of a desire to be disturbed in the middle of naps, dinner, or sex to help minimize the marketing costs of major corporations.

In fact, I was probably a charter member of what I refer to as the Do Not Fucking Call Me registry, and I resent when businesses like grocery store chains try to bribe phone numbers and other personal data out of us customers. I know better than to enter "contests" (thinly veiled data-sucks), and while I'll grudgingly apply for one of those "join your supermarket!" savings cards, I always sign up as "Mrs. Claus, Elf's Ass Lane, North Pole," with the phone number 1-555-1212—should anyone wish to call for information.

Even casual acquaintances know better than to dial my number on Monday and Tuesday when I'm on deadline for my column. Typically, I drag myself into the word quarry at 4 or 5 A.M. and stretch out my work day until 7 or 8 by periodically reviving myself with naps. Now, if you're a really, really good friend, and you're having a heart attack or similar dire emergency, by all means, call—that is, if you've first tried all your other friends, 911, the Auto Club, and that weird guy who gave you his card last night at the bar.

This being my attitude, the shrill ring of my phone late one Monday afternoon came as a surprise. Well, well, well . . . either somebody's getting read their last rites, or somebody's going to be. I glared hard at the phone. Failing to melt it, I was forced to answer it.

"Hello?"

"Hello-HELLO?"

Was anybody even there? Not exactly. It took a couple of seconds for the recording to start: "Hello, this is Tim Snee, vice president of Smart & Final . . ."

Oh, *is it*? Great. Because if you're phoning me at home in the middle of my deadline, there's an appropriate next line to your call, and it goes something like ". . . and someone's died and left you their townhouse in the center of Paris."

But, that wasn't Mr. Snee's message at all. Snee, I learned, was having some difficulty keeping shelves stocked at the warehouse store Smart & Final. He wanted to let his customers know they were working to solve the problem—lest anybody defect to Costco for their 100 packs of Charmin.

I took a moment to think about the checks I'd gotten recently. Nope, best I could recall, I hadn't received a single paycheck from Smart & Final, so I was pretty sure I wasn't in the employ of Tim

Snee. Yet, there he was, hijacking my time and the phone line I pay for to conduct his business.

Snee could've just sent me a letter—which I could either choose to read or use to clean up the little Tootsie Rolls my Yorkie drops. But, wait, that would incur printing and mailing costs. People would just have to deal. And, even if they are on the Do Not Call list, going after violators has got to be complicated. Who's gonna complain?

Yoohoo . . . Mr. Snee? You auto-dialed the wrong girl.

I got on the free people-finder site, Zabasearch.com, and typed in "Tim Snee" and "Timothy Snee." Bingo! There was a Timothy M. Snee in Long Beach, California. I dialed. A woman answered.

"Hello, Mrs. Snee?" I guessed. "This is Amy Alkon. I'm looking for Tim Snee—the Tim Snee who's a VP at Smart & Final." Yes, she said, he was her husband.

"Well, your husband called me at home, and I don't like that."

Silence. The kind you can hear. Poor lady. . . I imagined her imagining Tim crawling around on all fours in a hotel room, with me in a black leather bra and matching g-string, riding him and beating him with a black leather crop.

"I got this recorded message from your husband . . ." I said.

Now she got it. Sounding peeved, she explained that he was just letting people know they were working to correct the shelf-restocking problem.

Yeah, so I heard. "Guess what?" I snapped. "I don't work for Smart & Final or Tim Snee, and I resent getting calls from him at home. How do you like being bothered at home by some irritating stranger?"

Something told me she was underthrilled.

"Well, I don't like it either! I don't know Tim Snee, I don't want to know Tim Snee, and, most of all, I don't want Tim Snee bothering me at home. You tell your hubby to take my number off his list immediately, and never call me again!"

I slammed down the phone. Mmmmhmmm! That felt good. Yet, something was still missing: Compensation. Remuneration. Green, leafy CASH. Now, I know most people just sigh and hang up when they get a call like Snee's—which is why we all get calls like Snee's. My time and energy are valuable, and he'd just helped himself to both. I drafted a letter spelling out my disgust for Snee's business practices and invoicing him for $63.20, and e-mailed it to him:

> Tim,
> How dare you call me at home with a recorded
> message? I am on the Do Not Call list, and I value
> my privacy. I never gave Smart & Final my number
> or my permission to call me. How did you get it, by
> searching my credit card information? You woke
> me up in the middle of my nap during my deadline.
> Consider this an invoice for disturbing me: $63.20,
> which is my hourly rate for writing, since I'll probably
> lose at least an hour now thanks to your interruption.
> I'll now try to go back to sleep so I can get my
> writing done.

I'm considering reporting you to the California
Attorney General. I'm sure their fines for violating
the Do Not Call list are substantial. I hope so.
Have a bad day.
—Amy Alkon

While I was waiting for Snee's reply, I posted the story on my
blog—and included Mr. Snee's home phone number since he seems
to think it's okay to get calls from total strangers at home.

A few days later, I got this e-mail from Randall Oliver, Smart &
Final's "director of corporate communications":

Ms. Alkon:
I am very sorry that we disturbed you close to your
writing deadline. Our message was meant to provide
a helpful update to our customers, not to irritate
them. Nearly all of the responses we have received
have been very positive.

Really? Did other customers call you up and say, "I'm so lonely,
nothing makes my day like getting a recorded message smack in the
middle of my afternoon nap!"?

Oliver continued:

Our calling list was generated from information
provided to us by our customers on their

SmartAdvantage Card applications. We did not
obtain that information through any kind of intrusive
search. The service that transmits the voicemail
message checks all of the numbers against the
National Do Not Call Registry prior to sending the
message. We regret that your number was somehow
missed in that process . .

I filled in what he left out: ". . . because, unlike our other customers, who just lie down and take it, you're a major pain in the butt
cheeks!"

And finally, Oliver wrote:

We value you as a customer and hope to continue to
do business with you. We'd be happy to send you a
check for $63.20 as requested or alternatively would
be even happier to provide you a $100 Smart Card
for use at Smart & Final. Please let me know which
option you would prefer.

I'll take the $100—but, with a side of answers, Randall. You say
you got my number off a Smart & Final application, which probably
sounds plausible to you. As somebody who's extremely protective of
her personal and financial data, the likelihood that I'd write my real
name and phone number down is about on par with the odds that I'll
rocket out of bed at 3 A.M. to pitch a tent to get first crack at tickets to
NASCAR.

Oliver finally squeezed out a tale involving "somebody else" putting my home number down as their work number. Wow! Einstein would love that: all my digits randomly appearing in perfect order on somebody else's paperwork. What are the odds, 50 million to one? And, in another stunning coincidence, I shop at Smart & Final and use my credit card there—which ties to my billing address and phone number, yet that's not how they got my number?

I e-mailed Oliver again and again and asked to see the application. Whaddya know, I'm still waiting for my copy to arrive. In the meantime, I'm looking on the bright side: Not only did I get $100 worth of Snapple and fizzy water free, I know exactly where I'll turn should I ever be in the market for volume discounts on rotten eggs.

I had better results with another time-invader, the publishing house Bottom Line, which puts out a consumer affairs newsletter I subscribe to, covering, among other things, privacy rights! Surprise, surprise, they showed zero respect for mine. I'd just returned from a long trip, and I was jet-lagged out of my skull and way behind on my column. Desperate to get a few hours' rest, but increasingly convinced that I could actually be too tired to fall asleep, I spent an entire day flopping around on my couch like a big redheaded carp.

At 6 P.M., I finally nodded off. At 6:10 P.M., the phone rang. Did I want to take this opportunity to renew my Bottom Line subscription before it expired?

"Wha . . ."

Did I want to take this opportunity . . . ?

Yeah, that's exactly what I want to do. Right after I break into your bedroom at 3 A.M. and perch on the end of your bed crowing like a rooster. I slammed down the phone and spent the next six hours glaring at the ceiling and trying every sleep trick I could think of, from counting sheep to mentally chasing them down with an Uzi.

The next day, I was just as groggy and useless and just as unable to sleep. I finally keeled over at my new favorite bedtime of 6 P.M. Once again, Bottom Line rang me at 6:10. And, once again, at 6:11, I found myself too awake to sleep, not awake enough to write, and in no mood for "Law & Order" reruns.

Helloooo, Google!

Bottom Line, it turns out, does respect some privacy rights— their own. They're one of those companies that hides employee e-mail addresses in favor of general delivery accounts like "editorial"—meaning an e-mail might never reach Martin Edelston, Bottom Line's CEO and founder. I looked up Bottom Line's corporate address: Stamford, Connecticut. I figured there was a good chance the head honcho lived nearby. I hopped on Zabasearch and found a Martin Edelston at a couple of ritzy addresses in Greenwich. Unfortunately, the phone numbers weren't listed.

I addressed two envelopes to Edelston; one for each address. In each, I enclosed a copy of the blistering e-mail I sent to "editorial," arguing that having telemarketers harass his subscribers was rude, wrong, and just plain bad business. I included an invoice for $254.74 for use of my phone line, lost work hours thanks to my lost sleep, and for the two stamps it took to mail him my letters.

A week later, I got a package from Bottom Line with a couple of Bottom Line-published books, a Bottom Line T-shirt, and, most notably, an apology from Edelston, explaining that, thanks to me, he was reconsidering his company's use of telemarketers. I was impressed. Then, a week later, he sent another book—a pretty good one on business strategies he wrote himself—and a check for $254.74! I blogged the whole experience, hoping to inspire others to follow my lead and refuse to let corporations turn them into their tool.

When I called up Edelston in December of 2008 to see if Bottom Line was still telemarketing, I was disappointed to learn they were. Edelston told me they're "sensitive" about it, and "periodically reconsider" whether to keep doing it. But, he said, "We never get any complaints about it" (besides mine). This doesn't mean people aren't bothered, I told him. They're busy, have no idea who to call or what to say, and probably don't think their complaint will make any difference.

Still, I can see his point. While I'm far from the only one who hates having my life turned into a telephone sales call, as long as I'm the only one complaining and sending out invoices Edelston isn't likely to change his business practices. Consumers really are partly to blame for being such willing victims. By not speaking up, we tell businesses that a strict bottom-line approach is the most profitable, and hey, our phones are your phones!

Now, I know a lot of people think I'm nuts to respond to telemarketing calls the way I do. While I'm putting in some serious time chasing these jerks down—far beyond what it would take to simply hang up—that's me choosing how my time is spent; I'm not letting some golden-parachuted freeloader yank it away without my permission. Of course, my response pales compared to the hubris of executives who think it's perfectly acceptable to serially annoy 100,000 total strangers at home. And while the liberation from their home-invasion annoyance would be a prominent feature in my personal Utopia, there's a larger ethical issue here: How different is some executive who electronically breaks into your home and steals your time from some hood who physically breaks in and steals your TV? Theft is theft—even if the weapon being used to hold you up is your own telephone.

An executive who recognizes that it's wrong to steal from consumers is unlikely to become another Bernie Madoff or the Ken Lay behind the next Enron. As for the rest of them, when I call them at home to let them know "Eating dinner isn't just something I do while I'm waiting for your telemarketers to call," then throw in a bill, I'm putting them on notice that they're not untouchable; they will be held accountable. When it becomes this much trouble to steal what, to them, is probably 50 cents, maybe they'll be less likely to try to make off with $50 million. My motto: If, at first, you can't beat 'em, annoy the crap out of 'em, then bill 'em for your time!

HOW YOU CAN TURN JUNK CALLS INTO CASH

Turning a telemarketer's call into dollars—maybe even thousands of dollars—takes a lot less effort than you'd think. But, first things first. If, for some reason you've neglected to put your number on the national Do Not Call registry, hop to it. Call toll-free—1-888-382-1222—from the land line or mobile phone you want to register, or register online at donotcall.gov. Registration is free and remains effective for five years. Telemarketers are required to search the registry at least once every 31 days and scrub registered numbers from their lists of potential abusees. According to the site, after 31 days of being registered, you shouldn't get telemarketer calls. According to my experience, maybe not as many calls. When a call does come, you can file a complaint at donotcall.gov, and with your state attorney general. Or, you can just shake your fist really hard at the sky—which is probably about as effective.

Howling to the government about a telemarketer might make you feel better, but it's unlikely anyone will actually take action against the buggers. André-Tascha Lammé, webmaster of the anti-telemolestation site KillTheCalls.com, put in a Freedom of Information Act request to the Federal Trade Commission in 2006 and found that, of the almost three million complaints registered against telemarketers, the FTC and the Justice Department have brought a measly 25 cases. In the rare event the feds do go after one of these companies, you'll get nothing in return. For a more satisfying form of payback (the kind that actually pays you back) you have a couple of options.

While Junkbusters.com, JunkFax.org, JunkFaxes.org, DianaMey.com, KillTheCalls.com, and TCPATools.com are

(continued)

terrific resources for anybody interested in suing telemarketers or junk faxers, my preferred method is invoicing and annoying big corporate perps because I have more persuasive power in me than I do time and energy to haul my ass to Small Claims. Invoicing and annoying takes only documenting what company the telemarketer was calling for, finding some bigwig at that company, calling them (ideally, at home, if you can find that number), and sending a letter, fax, or e-mail asking them for compensation.

Invoicing also gets you around the loopholes that our lobbyist tools, uh, elected representatives, left in the Telephone Consumer Protection Act of 1991—as if a call from somebody wanting us to give our money to charity, which the TCPA allows, is less interruptive than one from somebody asking us to give it to Acme Carpet Cleaning. What's especially disgusting about "charity" calls is how little of the contributor's largesse goes to improving the lives of the poor and disenfranchised, and how much of it—sometimes 90 cents per dollar, according to CharityNavigator. org—goes to improving the yachts and private jets of the fat cats running telemarketing companies.

In addition to calls on behalf of tax-exempt nonprofits, the TCPA allows political calls, survey and market research calls, religious speech calls, and calls from companies with which you've had a previous business relationship (meaning a financial transaction within 18 months of the call). Also permitted are sales calls from somebody with whom you've had a "personal" relationship. So, yes, some drunk at the corner bar who sells magazine subscriptions can legally bug you by phone. The same goes for companies you've given permission to phone you— perhaps simply because you didn't read the fine print on that "contest" form you filled out for a "free" gym membership.

If you get a call from one of the loopholers, and you don't feel like invoicing, if nothing else, be sure to track down their home number on Zabasearch.com and call to survey them on why they think it's okay to call people at home and survey them. I'm sure they'll be thrilled, not only to hear from you but from 6,000 of your closest friends after you post their phone number on your blog or send it out in a mass e-mail.[35]

---

35 WARNING: Do this at your own risk, and only if a phone number is publicly available, or you may be accused of violating somebody's privacy for posting it. Call only once to avoid being accused of harassment.

The High Price Of Making Your Business My Business

If you're a businessman planning on having your telephone boiler room employees break into my life, you might first want to check out my rate card for that sort of thing, posted on my blog:

AMY ALKON'S PRICE LIST FOR TELEMARKETERS
Interrupting me during my nap: $3,012.50 (not
   including tax)
During dinner: $3,761.23
During sex: $13,456.50
   Other prices available upon request.

But, wait . . . isn't this a bit ridiculous? As a corporate executive using telemarketing, should you really be expected to search my blog for a price list? I mean, how do you even know I have a blog? Well, you wouldn't walk into a restaurant and order lunch without knowing the price, would you? Before your company calls me, you'd better do your homework. Don't just assume you can turn my dinnertime into a data-mining session, gambling that I, like so many others, will let you use my time and my telephone line for free.

That's what market research company GfK Automotive tried to do, just after I sat down to dinner. When the phone rang, I figured it was my boyfriend calling from Detroit to tell me what plane he was coming in on. I leapt up and made a run for the phone, scattering my silverware and terrifying my little Yorkie, who narrowly missed being impaled by my fork.

Crap. The phone wasn't in my office. The bathroom! I'd left it in the bathroom. I dashed through my bedroom, stubbing my toe on a big book I'd left on the floor. Cringing from the pain, I grabbed the phone and finally answered the call—which wasn't even for me. Sure, the woman on the other end said she was calling to talk to me, and even asked for me by name, but once again, only because surveying me by electronic home invasion is cheaper than doing the polite thing, sending a letter to ask me whether I'd like to participate.

Here's my initial e-mail to GfK, addressed to "Eileen"—some poor former employee GfK left listed on their website as a PR contact, leading me to call her at home. (Sorry, Eileen. Better luck next company!)

> Eileen,
>
> Per my call Tuesday night to *your* home phone number about the annoying phone call I got from your company at my home, here is the invoice for my time and usage of my phone line for your GfK automotive survey (I was called approximately 6 P.M., Tuesday, January 31, by one of your junk phoners): $50, payable immediately.
>
> Taking my time and using my phone line without my permission so you can scare up some free data is parasitism and theft. Do not call me again. Please let me know how soon I can expect your company's check. I strongly suggest you do business more ethically in the future—by hiring people to give you the information you need instead of trying to get a free ride off people like me.
>
> —Amy Alkon

In response, I got the "go away, silly girl" treatment from GfK honcho Don DeVeaux, who e-mailed to inform me that GfK had gotten my number through "standard industry practice." Really? Well, Don, it used to be "standard practice" to have a house full of slaves. DeVeaux then blew off his company's intrusion into my life by informing me that it was legal for them to call me because they were surveying me, not selling me something. True, Don. But, even if it was legal, as I pointed out to him—by e-mail and in a rambling message I left on *his* home phone—that doesn't mean it's free. Here's the response I e-mailed to DeVeaux (co-written by the angry eighth-grader in me):

Don,

Regardless of whether this is legal (and I would suspect a case could be brought since this isn't a political survey, you are selling something—the data obtained), your concern should be whether it's ethical business behavior.

I am on the Do Not Call registry, as, I'm sure, are many people you called. Do you really think I registered for that list, and then said, "Oh, goody, I can still have auto marketing companies bug me at dinner time on a phone line I pay for"? Apparently, you really don't give a damn what anyone wants, as long as you can play parasite/host within the letter of the law.

I'm a capitalist, and I believe in compensating people for their time and equipment, and by using my time and equipment without my permission you are stealing from me, and it's disgusting. Forget whether you pay for the survey, if taken. You have to pay to disturb me at all.

Your "intent" was not to inconvenience me? Again, you clearly don't give a damn whether you do, or you wouldn't be calling me or anyone else at home, on phone lines we pay for—an apparent attempt to offload your research costs on the public. So, let's dispense with the pretense of politeness. You're not polite; you're just getting away with as much as you can without being prosecuted.

Now, I've called *you* at home. I'm sure you were excited and charmed.

Do give me a list of all your friends and their home numbers and I'll call them, too, and survey them on where they stand on this issue. Don't ask them for their permission or anything. I'll just interrupt them on the phone lines they pay for, regardless of whether they want to be interrupted. Why? Because *I* feel like it. Because it's good for ME! Me, Me, Me! What about them, their feelings, their needs, their desire not to be disturbed? Oh, not important, because it's legal to call them. Get my point?

You owe me $50. I will up the amount if I have to do substantially more e-mailing to you. The big question: Will people behave ethically and courteously if the law doesn't directly force them to do so? Will you?

—Amy Alkon

Note that I only invoiced GfK for the discounted price of $50 (a considerable savings over my abusive telemarketer rack rate of $3,761.23). The truth is, I'm not looking to gouge anybody. I purposely kept the dollar figure low to make it easier for DeVeaux to see his way to paying me. Sending me $50 would be an acknowledgment that the company had no right to use my time and my telephone equipment without compensation. Ideally, the check would have been accompanied by an apology from DeVeaux and a pledge to reconsider the ethics of petty theft by telephone.

Until lawmakers cut out the cute loopholes they've left in the telemarketing law, stopping telephonic home invasion will be left to those of us who not only track, invoice, and threaten to sue some CEO, but leave long-winded complaints on his home answering machine. Which reminds me . . . Don! Don DeVeaux! You might rethink having your kid do your outgoing message.

When Push Comes to Sue

Because DeVeaux never responded to my e-mail or paid my invoice, I realized I had to follow through and sue. When I think of taking somebody to court, I picture myself as one of those hot prosecutor girls on "Law & Order," strutting across the courtroom in stiletto pumps to put some scumbag away: "Yes, Mr. Telemarketer, you've interrupted your last dinner. 20-to-life!"

The reality was, I didn't have the slightest idea of how to go about suing, and the prospect of actually appearing in court made me queasy. But, a girl's gotta do what a girl's gotta do. I dragged myself on to the Los Angeles Small Claims Court website, and discovered that the first step was sending DeVeaux a "letter of demand" asking for payment. Okay, in my case, a snotty letter of demand:

> I am now demanding the entire $3,761.23 dinner interruption/use-of-my-telephone-equipment fee, payable to me within four business days from receipt of this e-mail. That would be Monday, January 28. I'm assuming you'll send it Federal Express. Feel free to deduct the cost of overnighting it to me from $3,761.23. (I know, I'm a sport!)
>
> If I do not receive full payment of the $3,761.23 within the above-mentioned time frame, I will be forced to bring suit against you in Small Claims Court in Los Angeles County for that sum. Note: Per the Supreme Court's ruling in the "International Shoe" case, I am entitled to sue here rather than coming to Detroit. Just so you know!

As you can see from the International Shoe reference (a 1945 Supreme Court decision I learned about from a lawyer in a coffee shop), I immersed myself in the law in preparation for my case—about up to my ankles. I knew just enough to be a danger to myself in court, but hoped I sounded at least a little worrisome to DeVeaux and company. As for the short payment schedule I allowed, I hoped it made me seem like a hardass. The truth? I so dreaded suing that I waited until the last possible minute to file, just days before the two-year statute of limitations ran out.

I had three months between filing and my court appearance, and I used every moment of this time to procrastinate wildly. The day before my court date, I called André-Tascha Lammé in a panic. Lammé, a Sacramento-based bleeding-heart conservative who's always working about three community causes and about as many jobs, started the site KillTheCalls.com after he was deluged with telemarketing calls from mortgage companies. He asked them to stop. And asked, and asked, and asked. And when the calls kept coming—dozens and dozens a day—he got mad, got on the Internet, and discovered that he could get his life back and maybe make some pretty good money in the process.

On his site, he estimates that he spent five hours, total, on four cases against telemarketers, and grossed $6,160. Subtract his expenses ($250, mostly for filing fees and process-serving), and it works out to $1,182 per hour. Best of all, he only had to go to court once, in the one case a telemarketer refused to settle. Not bad, huh? In fact, for that hourly rate, it would be my pleasure to listen to just about any sales pitch anybody wants to make. And hey, speak slowly! Enunciate! Don't leave out a single detail!

Lammé told me not to worry; it was unlikely GfK would show up. After all, they're a big international company with headquarters in Detroit, New York, and Switzerland. Were they really going to ship a lawyer to Santa Monica over a measly three grand? Well, it was possible, so I thought I'd better do my homework—college-midterm style, since I was then just hours away from my court date.

I was awake much of that night, hunting legal loopholes on the Internet. Federal law didn't have the answer, and neither did a host of anti-telemarketing websites, so I moved on to California law; specifically, the Business and Professions Code—a real page-turner. Finally, at around 1 P.M., when my case seemed to be very much in the dumpster, I found them—exactly the sections I needed. Relieved, I typed up my case and photocopied documents. I slept for a few hours, pulled my hair into a tight bun, donned the most conservative blazer and skirt I had, wrapped my shaking hands around my steering wheel and drove to the courthouse.

In the courtroom, I kept swiveling my head to look for formidable looking international businessmen in stern glasses and serious suits. Nope. Just ordinary Southern Californians, mostly with still-wet hair and clothes entirely inappropriate for court. The girl next to me had a roommate who owed her money. The guy on the other side owed somebody on his payday loan. Both told me they hated telemarketers and were glad I was suing.

The bailiff called my name. "Here!" I answered. I clenched my knees together hard, waiting for the moment I could breathe a sigh of relief and get up and go home, victorious by default. "GfK Automotive?" the bailiff called. Whoops, what's that? Somebody spoke up. I whipped around. In the back of the courtroom, a slight, sandy-haired guy in a business shirt, no tie, motioned to the bailiff. Oh, no. They'd actually sent somebody.

The guy turned out to be Josh Spector, GfK's New York–based corporate counsel, their vice-president for legal affairs.[36] Great. I was a love advice columnist doing my best to look lawyerish. The bailiff told all the plaintiffs and defendants to go out in the hall and exchange documents. I introduced myself to Spector, then asked

---

36 Amy at the Los Angeles Small Claims Advisory Program said that attorneys normally are not allowed in Small Claims but may represent a company if they are regular employees or officers of the company, as long as they're not being paid beyond their regular salary for their court appearance.

whether he enjoyed being disturbed at home by telemarketers. He told me GfK was within the bounds of the law, and if I had a problem with telemarketing, I should contact my congressman. I could practically hear his eyes roll as he spoke. Arrogant fuck. Can't my life belong to me without my petitioning for somebody to pass legislation saying so?

I handed him a copy of my packet—20 pages of color-coded, indexed, highlighted documents—and asked for a copy of his. Uh, actually, he'd only brought a copy for himself and another for the judge—just one page, probably containing the passage from federal telemarketing law about market research calls being allowed. I smiled. Big-time New York lawyer doesn't read the court rules? "You can't give the judge a document if you don't have a copy for me, too," I told him. He frowned and said he'd just read from it. Heh, heh . . . you do that, Clarence Darrow.

Back in the courtroom, I kept turning around to see what the Joshster was making of my packet. He didn't even appear to be looking at it. Did he think he had that much of a slam dunk? Finally, our case got called. The judge was Rex H. Minter, a former Santa Monica mayor. He was pretty old, with white hair and hang-dog eyes, and a frown that suggested he was ready to throw the book at somebody. I hoped it wouldn't be me.

Spector and I stood at adjacent tables while the judge went through my packet. He didn't just flip through. He took his time, actually reading my documents. I looked over at Josh. He was—rather feverishly, it seemed—pawing through my packet. Smart move, Josh! The judge seems interested. Who knows, maybe there's something of value in all those pages!

I began presenting my case against GfK. The judge broke in, asking me how many of these cases against telemarketers I'd brought before. I knew what he was getting at. There are opportunists who file suit after suit against telemarketers who've violated the law, turning suing them into an alternate way of making a living. I'm not one of them, but I don't feel sorry for the telemarketers getting sued. The telemarketers, however, sure do get indignant when people try to collect on their violations. André-Tascha told me that telemarketers he went after called him a "sue-happy scumbag," and accused him of "just being in it for the money" (as if they're tele-harassing people just for the *luvvvvv*!).

I told the judge it was my first case ever. I explained that I'm not a litigious person, and I wouldn't have brought it to court if they'd given me $50 when I invoiced them, affirming that they weren't allowed to steal my time and use of my phone line. I actually would've made out much better, time- and energy-wise, if I'd just taken their damn survey (of hybrid car owners,[37] in this case), because they were offering $250 for doing it. But, for me, it really is about the principle—refusing to be victimized by people who turn a bigger profit by bothering other people in their homes. The moment a telemarketer calls me, there's a price to pay, set by me. The fact that few others charge when they're bothered, and that my price is unexpected by the telemarketers—well, really not my problem. Interrupt my dinner, get invoiced. It's as simple as that.

---

37 Kudos to my Honda dealer, who thanked me for the largest purchase I've ever made in my life by selling my contact information to jerks who sold it to jerks who would interrupt my dinner.

Shockingly, Mr. Hotshot New York Lawyer didn't even seem to have the details about his company's call to me. Apparently, he thought he'd make quick work of me, simply by saying GfK was a surveyor, not a telemarketer, and quoting one line from the telemarketing code to make his case—that the business of abuse is a-okay by law just as long as the perps are doing market research. Not so fast, lawyer-man. I asked the judge to open my packet to the yellow tag-indexed page, California Business and Professions Code, section 17529-529.9. I took pleasure in drawing out the full name and section number; my way of saying to snide Joshiepoo, "Whoops, looks like the little lady did her homework!"

This section is actually about spammers, but discussed what they called "cost-shifting," sticking the recipient of a commercial message with the cost of sending it, a practice which sucks more than $10 billion a year from U.S. organizations in lost productivity and spam-combating equipment and software. I drew a parallel to the business of home invasion by telephone, noting that I do not maintain phone service to make GfK's data-gathering costs cheaper. Yet, solely for the betterment of their bottom line, they seized use of my equipment without my permission—perhaps cutting off access to a caller I did want to hear from; maybe an editor wanting to hire me. And it wasn't just *my* equipment they were seizing use of. They're actually in the business of abuse, doing the same to legions of consumers across California.

To shut down Josh's "we were just market-researching" defense, I pulled out my star loophole, California Business and Professions Code section 17590-594, and set about redefining GfK as telemarketers—which would, in turn, make them law violators whenever they call somebody on the Do Not Call list.

According to that part of the code, a telephone solicitor (i.e., a telemarketer) is somebody who uses the phone to "offer a prize or to rent, sell, exchange, promote, gift, or lease goods or services or documents that can be used to obtain goods or services." I reminded the judge that GfK had offered me $250 to participate in their survey—a cash prize! Which makes them . . . telephone solicitors! Which makes them liable for my full rate-card fee of $3,761.23 for interrupting my dinner! What, Josh? What's that funny noise, you ask? Sounds rather like the canary swallowing the cat, don't you think?

I tossed in a few more points to bolster my case. There was subsection C, which says a telephone solicitor is somebody who "seeks marketing information that will or may be used for the direct . . . sale of goods or services" to the person they're calling. Josh objected. He said they don't do that. All well and good that he says so, I told the judge. But how could I possibly trust people who are in the business of abuse to protect my privacy?

Besides, I told the judge, there really was no valid reason for GfK to take my time and use my phone line without my say-so. I quoted from subsection F, which said "Nothing in this section prohibits a telephone solicitor from contacting" a person by mail to ask for permission to call them. Nothing, I noted, but being too damn cheap.

For my grand finale, explaining why GfK should pay me the entire $3,761.23 I charge telemarketers for disturbing my dinner, I turned to the Grilled Cheese Defense: "If the gentleman from GfK went to a restaurant where there were no prices posted and ordered a grilled cheese sandwich, and it turned out to cost $45, he'd still have to pay for it."

The judge excused us and said we'd get his decision in the mail. Just a few days later, the judgment came. I couldn't believe it. I'd won—beaten a huge company and a guy who lawyers for a living. I was a little disappointed at the amount—only $50 plus court costs; a total of $120, instead of the $3,761.23 I'd asked for. I think I should have the freedom to charge whatever price I want for my time, and a company like GfK has a choice: don't use my services, or pay the price I set for them. Who knows, maybe Judge Minter will one day see it my way, maybe some night as he sits down to dinner, and keeps sitting down to dinner—when the phone keeps ringing and ringing and it's always for his wallet.

9

MODEMS WITHOUT MANNERS

I am not one of those hairy-toed neo-hippies who's renounced indoor plumbing and White Cloud for a stack of leaves next to a freshly dug toilet hole in the backyard. I don't think our lives would be better if only we could go back to a simpler time, before nasty developments like running water, the History Channel, and reliable birth control. In fact, for me, communing with nature means walking down a city sidewalk with grass growing up between the cracks, and camping is staying in a hotel that doesn't give you Aveda toiletries and a lighted magnifying mirror. As somebody who is decidedly not into premodern inconveniences, you could say I not only appreciate technology, I worship it. Still, I get that advanced technology often brings with it advanced side effects.

Just a couple decades ago, there was no such thing as an instant message; there was only the rather delayed message, chiseled out in longhand or typed on a typewriter and painstakingly corrected with cross-outs or Wite-Out. After getting it down on the page, you'd have to find your address book, dig up your recipient's information, find an envelope and a stamp . . . you know the drill. Maybe a week later, the postman would deliver your message. Because corresponding took time, supplies, and effort, you didn't write just anything to just anybody; for example, it's unlikely you would've mailed somebody you'd never even met a letter informing them "I told you to stay the fuck out of my inbox, you lowlife, dried-up twat."

That message came to me by e-mail from a total stranger after an exchange in which I responded, rather politely, to a rather minor criticism he'd e-mailed me about one of my advice columns. Thanks to the growth of the Web and the affordability of computers, he and billions of other ordinary people suddenly found themselves in possession of the extraordinary ability to lash out at others extremely fast, practically free, and with very little effort.

That said, the Internet has changed my life and so many people's in amazingly positive ways, and it would be stupid (and futile) to suggest we turn back the clock. I'd just like to shine a light on a few areas where the global village seems to be populated by a bunch of club-wielding troglodytes, and see if we all can make an effort to bring a little more civility to the place.

In a column in the summer of 2008, I wrote a response to a girl who signed herself "Chicken." She wanted to dump her boyfriend using Slydial, a service that sends calls to a mobile phone straight to voice mail. "Chicken" had been dating the guy for five months and longing to break up for two, but said she'd been stalling because she didn't have the guts to hurt him. The core of my response was this:

So, two months ago, you knew it was over, but instead of ending it, you let him get two months more attached. Maybe you wanted to avoid hurting him, but, clearly, what you wanted even more was to avoid feeling awkward while hurting him. If you've dated somebody for any length of time, it's cruel to dismiss them with a phone message. You owe it to this guy to end it face to face.

A reader, whose name I'll change to "Kevin Jones," took issue with my response, but signed his e-mail "Respectfully," a conciliatory touch suggesting he had some manners.

Amy,
I think you seriously missed the boat on this one. The only, sole purpose and reason for being of SlyDial is to accommodate C-O-W-A-R-D-S.

It is by far much more cruel and egotistical to string someone along (for 2 months!) then to be open and honest about it so that the poor guy would have known where he stood with him/her.

You should have hammered Chicken as the gutless wonder that he/she was and is.
Respectfully,
—Kevin

I wrote back:

Dear Kevin,

Thanks, but I made that point—that she let him get two months more attached. And per Adam Smith, "The Theory of Moral Sentiments," evoking sympathy is probably the best way to motivate somebody. It's a hammering, but more effective than just making her defensive. Anyway, thanks for the e-mail and for reading me.

Best,

—Amy

"Kevin" and "Respectfully" had apparently parted ways:

Wow,

You've lost just any credibility you might have had— quoting a book from 1759. What a load of crap.[38]

It's no wonder we only see your scratching-the-bottom-of-the-barrel drivel online[39] (cheap!) instead of print.

—KEVIN JONES

---

38 Hilariously, Mr. Old Info Is Worthless had this quote from the long-dead John Adams at the bottom of every e-mail he sent me: "In my many years I have come to a conclusion that one useless man is a shame, two is a law firm, and three or more is a congress."

39 That particular paper runs my column in their online edition only.

Nasty. And surprising, since the guy's e-mail included his full name, e-mail address, home address, home phone number, cell phone number, and his website—more information than I usually see from anybody but PR people. I could've let the guy's nastiness go unremarked, but to me, that's tacitly condoning it. I wrote back:

> Wow. First of all, how rude.
>
> Secondly, are you really of the opinion that because books are old they are valueless? Do you likewise think the work of Aristotle and Shakespeare are shit?
>
> Are you typically a mean guy, or did you maybe have a bad day and decide that trying to be hurtful to me would be a way to make yourself feel better?
> —Amy Alkon

I knew what was coming. Usually, when I make that last point— why lash out at me?—the reader writes back, all embarrassed, and apologizes. In fact, I can almost count on it. Kevin, it turns out, was an exception:

> Oh, sweet Jesus—you tired old cunt.
>
> You haven't seen or heard rude, yet.
>
> I'm in touch with the publisher of the paper—a personal friend—regarding your asinine behavior.
>
> Get some treatment, toots, FAST!—you need it desperately.

Well, that, and extensive plastic surgery, according to another e-mail-equipped troglodyte who dashed off his thoughts of me and hit "send":

> Hey
> Whats that black thing crawling up your neck,
> looking like it wants to overtake your chin? Oh,
> thats a Turtleneck??? Whoo wears those anymore?
> In summertime? Im not sure you have the kind of
> face you want framed liked that anyway. You might
> want to have that birdcage liner paper post up a
> fresh pic. But I do enjoy your [column] once in awhile
> when I dont feel like poneying up .50 cents for a real
> newspaper. It must make ya feel good being quen of
> the idiots.
> —Derek M.

Yet another trog wasn't satisfied with sending me nasty e-mail; he anonymously signed me up for a slew of Internet mailing lists—about 30 of them—everything from the John Birch Society to the NRA to Omaha Steaks and some lobster company.

Unluckily for him, I decided it would be wrong to delete these messages as spam since the companies didn't actually spam me. (Getting deemed a spammer can cause subsequent messages to subscribers to get trapped in spam filters.) It was a pain, but I set about unsubscribing my e-mail address from every mailing list—and, to my surprise, was rewarded for my effort.

7:20 PM	sparklist-confirm-15...	Your confirmation is needed
7:22 PM	lyris-noreply@listserv...	Welcome to the Townhall.com Opinion A...
7:23 PM	membership@heritag...	You have been added to the MyHeritage
7:27 PM	sub-all@jbs.org	Confirmation
7:27 PM	sub-all@jbs.org	Confirmation
7:27 PM	Fair@fairus.org	Thank You For Registering with FAIR
7:29 PM	lyris-confirm-12815...	Your confirmation is needed
7:37 PM	whitehouse-lists-conf...	Your Confirmation is Needed
7:38 PM	custserv@omahastea...	" Omaha Steaks Confirmation...Thank Y
7:40 PM	lobsters-help@lists.m...	confirm subscribe to lobsters@lists.mai
7:40 PM	tx22.ima.pub@mail.h...	Thank you for Subscribing to Legislati
7:43 PM	lyris-noreply@listserv...	Welcome to TownHall.com's What's New
7:43 PM	lyris-noreply@listserv...	Re: townhall-alert
7:43 PM	lyris-noreply@listserv...	Welcome to the Townhall.com Conserv
7:43 PM	lyris-noreply@listserv...	Re: your subscribe request
7:44 PM	JunkScience@lib.bcent...	Welcome to JunkScience.com
7:45 PM	alansears@alliancedef...	Email News -- Requires Confirmation
7:47 PM	email_news_alert@bu...	Welcome to the Exxon Mobil Corporati
7:57 PM	info@nraila.org	Thank you for signing up for NRA-ILA
8:07 PM	newsletter@all.org	Thank you for joining the new ALL new
8:19 PM	lyris-noreply@listserv...	Re: your unsubscribe request
8:23 PM	custserv@omahastea...	We have removed your email address.
8:24 PM	lyris-noreply@listserv...	Re: your unsubscribe request
8:24 PM	lyris-noreply@listserv...	Re: your unsubscribe request
8:26 PM	lobsters-help@lists.m...	confirm unsubscribe from lobsters@li:
8:27 PM	lobsters-help@lists.m...	ezmlm response

(Delete) (Save to ⬦)

Screen shot of my e-mail box.

On one of the unsubscribe pages, up popped a short string of numbers and the message "The IP address you subscribed from" (meaning "Internet Protocol," the unique numerical address of a particular computer). Bingo!

I ran a search of that IP,[40] which traced back to an Adelphia subscriber. Since the IP finder didn't list the subscriber's name or email, all I could do was report my spammer to abuse@ adelphia.com. And, I noticed an unopened e-mail in my inbox—one that came just before all the subscription notices.

I opened it and looked for the IP. Yep, shore enough, it was the guy who subscribed me to the newsletters. It seems he was steamed about an article I'd written critical of unnecessary SUV driving—aircraft-carrier-sized gas-guzzlers that aren't being used by contractors to haul steel beams across town, but by Hollyweasels, to ferry around a script and a latte. Here's an excerpt from his e-mail:

---

40 On arin.net/whois/

I just bought my wife a HUGE Suburban. Lovely, 11 miles to the gallon in the city! MMMMM! As for me, I just can't give up my 1973 Jeep and 2002 Ford 250!!!! I had a 2001 Corvette but just got tired of it—sorry! When my kids are 18, they get whatever they want as long as it has a V8! Ahhhh, Capitalism!!!!! Support the economy that has given us all so much!!!! RJ p.s. Don't fret, someday you will get laid and find something worth while to occupy your time with instead of vulgar insults! Oh, and please remember, always Give War a Chance!

This proud supporter of OPEC signed his e-mail with his initials only, so I took a closer look at the section of the e-mail with the IP and other technogibberish. Most helpfully (and probably unbeknownst to him), it happened to include his company name. I hopped on Google, and in about 20 minutes rounded up his full name, website, and cell phone number, which I called, pronto. After he recovered from the shock of it being me on the line, I chewed him out and told him he had to be accountable for what he'd done.

He just kept saying he was sorry. Not good enough, I told him. He'd taken my time, and he owed me for it. I asked for $50. The guy bragged that he charges $250 an hour (classy!) and said he'd send me the $50 in "a couple weeks." Right. After I hung up, I typed out a blog item about our encounter, speculating as to whether he'd pay me, and posted it before I went to bed. The next morning, the first comment was from him:

Good morning all—I am the inconsiderate jack@ss.
No excuse for my actions, suffice to say, I will put my
money where my apology is for Amy's time ASAP.

And he did. The guy actually came through!

The small print on the envelope says "True to my word!"

Again, in pursuing these Web-powered offenders, I know I'm going against the conventional wisdom that when the going gets nasty it's best to not engage; or, as George Bernard Shaw[41] put it, " . . . never to wrestle with a pig. You get dirty, and besides, the pig likes it." Well, I'm not afraid of getting dirty. And every time I pig-wrestle some Internet jerk, I'm telling them, "You didn't just send your meanness off into the nebulousphere. There's an actual person on the other end." And just maybe, by doing that, I can persuade a pig or two to move out of the sty; perhaps to a cozy little one-bedroom apartment.

---

41 Attributed to Shaw.

Why Stab Somebody When You Can
Mouse-Click Them To Death?

While I'm opposed to gratuitous meanness, I'm probably less sensitive than most to insults or criticism; probably because I seek out criticism (from those I respect), and, because I'm a newspaper columnist and blogger, insults manage to find their way to me without my help. I don't think it's wrong to use snarky humor to criticize people; that is, when somebody seems guilty of something beyond having a big nose or a weak chin. But, far too many Internet interactions play out like *Mean Girls*, except the mean girls aren't always girls. A number of them are middle-aged women.

In Missouri, in 2006, according to news reports of a tragic, twisted Cyrano story,[42] 49-year-old Laurie Drew,[43] her 18-year-old assistant, Ashley Grills, and Drew's 13-year-old daughter used a fake MySpace identity to torment Megan Meier, a depressed and socially struggling 13-year-old. Posing as a 16-year-old boy named "Josh," they

---

42 ABC News, *The New York Times*, Wired, *Spartanburg Herald-Journal*, and Associated Press.

43 Kim Zetter reported in Wired that Drew's hairdresser, Christina Chu, testified that Drew had boasted that she'd worked with her assistant to set up the MySpace profile to get back at Meier. Drew, through her attorney, has denied creating or directing anyone to create the MySpace account, but said she was aware of it. Drew also denies sending any of the messages to Meier. This contradicts the testimony of Corporal Edwin Lutz, of the St. Charles County Sheriff's Department. Wired's Zetter reports that Lutz testified that Drew told him just weeks after Meier's death that "she had contributed to (Meier's suicide) by creating a MySpace account," and that she, Grills, and her daughter had all communicated with Meier through that account.

befriended Meier, reportedly hoping to get evidence to back up their suspicion that she'd been gossiping about Drew's daughter. When Meier eventually pressed to meet the nonexistent Josh, Grills, as Josh, tried to shut down their exchange by turning on her and taunting her, e-mailing Meier that the world would be a better place without her. Meier hanged herself in her bedroom closet.

Prosecutors in Missouri, where the e-mail to Meier originated, declined to charge Drew for cyber-bullying, saying no laws had been broken, but a grand jury in Los Angeles, where MySpace has its servers, indicted Drew in May of 2008. The charge, ABC's Scott Michaels reported, was "conspiracy and unauthorized access to a protected computer with the intent to get information to cause emotional distress, a felony." Grills was granted immunity in exchange for testifying against Drew.

In November 2008, Drew was found guilty of three counts of unauthorized access to MySpace, reduced from felonies to misdemeanors by the jury, which apparently rejected the prosecution's contention that Drew intended to harm Meier. The jury deadlocked on the criminal conspiracy count, and U.S. District Judge George Wu declared a mistrial on that charge. In July 2009, Wu threw out the verdicts against Drew. According to the Associated Press, Wu said that if Drew were found guilty of illegally accessing computers, anyone who ever violated a social networking site's terms of service would be guilty of a misdemeanor. That, he said, would be unconstitutional.

Meier's mother has created a foundation in her daughter's name and speaks at schools to increase awareness about the potential costs of cyber-bullying.[44] On meganmeierfoundation.org, she quotes Megan's father, who concedes that it was ultimately Megan's choice to kill herself, "but, it was like somebody handed her a loaded gun."

Usually, malice on the Web doesn't lead to physical death, just death to reputation. And what better way for a guy to find out about his than in a call from his momma, who also happens to be a minister, asking him whether it's true he has an STD? A friend of hers had spotted the guy's photo with the warning, *"DO NOT DATE HIM. He gave me an STD and dated 2 people at a time,"* on dontdatehimgirl. com, a site where women anonymously post nasty allegations about men they've dated.[45]

In addition to the STD accusation, other dontdatehimgirl postings about the guy, a Pittsburgh attorney, were "he wears dirty clothes," "complains about paying child support," "heard he was gay," and "he got hookups in every zip code." The guy filed suit against the site in Pennsylvania. The Electronic Frontier Foundation (eff.org), a defender of digital civil liberties, urged the court to dismiss his claim, arguing for the protection of the free flow of information online. EFF's Rebecca Jeschke wrote on their site, "It's important to note that the claims against the people who posted the messages in the first place

---

44 *USA Today.*

45 Similar sites include the now-defunct playersandpsychos.com ("where players get played & psychos get spayed") and truedater.com, featuring post-date reviews of people with profiles on online dating sites.

still stand. If any defamation occurred, it's the speakers who should bear the responsibility, not the soapbox."

The guy did post rebuttals, but it's near impossible to reverse the damage that's been done. As with those tiny corrections buried in the newspaper after they, say, scramble a few letters and accidentally finger some innocent person as a child molester, once an accusation's out there, it's pretty much out there. Making matters worse, it's common for people to Google the name of anyone they're considering dating or doing business with. So, thanks to these anonymous postings about the Pittsburgh attorney, he appears to be at once gay and a womanizer, dirty and diseased, and if that's not enough to send potential dates and business prospects packing, he's reported to be a bad dad, to boot. In the words of the accused in a comment on a *Wall Street Journal* blog item about his case, "You cant (sic) imagine that what you have worked so hard for all your life could be jeapordized (sic) or questioned not by the stroke of the pen but by the key board."

Lord Of The Fleas

With the popularity of blogs comes a new kind of Web bullying—the Web mob, dispatched by a popular blog or website to infest the blog or website of somebody the blogger or bloggers dislike or disagree with. Although I'm neither left nor right (I describe myself as fiscally conservative, socially libertarian, and a "personal responsibilitarian"), I became one of the pet targets of a blog that exists to attack conservatives.

These self-proclaimed "progressives" who went after me don't just dispute offending ideas; they use their blog to denigrate the person who had them. I find that pretty junior high, but not a big deal. What

I take issue with is the way they use their blog (which I'm not going to promote by naming) to incite the Web version of throwing rotten eggs: sending over hordes of "tiny little thugs," as I came to call them, all anonymous, to post hundreds of inane and abusive comments on their target's website.

Their attacks on me came after I blogged about an Ohio woman named Tarika Wilson; at 26, she was the mother of six children, ages one to eight, fathered by five different drug dealers. Wilson was still dating the latest of these drug dealers when she was shot and killed in a SWAT raid when the police came to serve a warrant on him at her house.

According to reports in *The Lima News* and *The Toledo Blade*, that boyfriend, Anthony Terry, 31, had previously been convicted of numerous crimes. He'd once tried to wrestle a police officer's gun from him, and had nearly been shot to death in a violent argument with another man. In the raid on Wilson's house, pot, bullets, drug money, a baggy of crack cocaine, and a digital scale with drug residue were reportedly recovered, and Terry was arrested. An Ohio jury subsequently found the officer, who shot at the "shadowy figure" who turned out to be Wilson, not guilty of misdemeanor negligent homicide and negligent assault charges.

Now, I don't like our drug laws, I think it's horrible that Wilson was killed, and I find it reprehensible to execute a SWAT raid on a house with six children in it, but that wasn't what I focused on. As I wrote in my blog item:

> . . . the police generally don't seek to break down
> the doors of homes of women who've had five

boyfriends who are all, say, accountants, architects, or managers at Subway.

It's awful that this woman was killed, but the fact remains: Lie down with drug dealers, wake up with drug raids.

Also, in researching my advice column, I've done a lot of reading on what gives kids the best shot in this world (or even an adequate shot), and I've come to the very un-PC conclusion that kids need daddies and intact families; or in the case of gay and lesbian parents, per the research of NYU sociologist Judith Stacey and others, two loving parents in an intact family.

Not only did Wilson bring numerous daddyless children into the world, her children were also mommyless when she spent 372 days in prison on a 2004 drug charge for driving yet another one of her Mr. Wonderfuls to a park where he sold 237 grams of crack cocaine to a confidential informant.

There was one major problem with what I blogged. The woman, Tarika Wilson, was black, and I'm white. In certain circles, if a white person dares to criticize a black person, or point out a problem in the black community, it's automatically seen as racism. Never mind what all the statistics say; for example, about the color of single motherhood, which is far too often black, with 68.8 percent of black American children born out of wedlock versus 26.7 percent of white children, according to a 2000 U.S. Department of Health and Human Services survey. A Department of Labor-funded survey found that black children, on average, spent 49.4 percent of their lives in single-parent homes, as opposed to 12.8 percent for white children.

I get that Wilson, and many poor black women, haven't had the opportunities I've had, and I realize that discrimination against blacks certainly continues, but I don't think there's any excuse for bringing multiple fatherless children into poverty. I decided to say something—not because I'm racist, but because I think it's racist to hold some women to a lower standard because they happen to be black.

So, in my blog item, I wrote about how terrible and tragic I think it is that so many black children keep growing up poor and daddyless, and how I think the lack of stigma for teen motherhood and unwed motherhood in general in the black community helps perpetuate that. Most mystifyingly, activists like Jesse Jackson, who supposedly has the best interests of the black community at heart, never get around to holding prayer vigils or protest marches outside the houses of single mothers who've had six children with various drug dealers and bring home the latest of those drug dealers for regular dinners and sleepovers.

Can We Talk About My Penis?

You don't have to agree with me about Tarika Wilson or anything else. You can disagree with me, consider me an idiot or worse, and I'll welcome you to come to my blog and tell me why you think so. But, hey, why debate me on the points of an issue when you can send over a mob to attack me for my looks and speculate about my sexuality and gender? After I posted my entry on Tarika Wilson, the "progressives" posted two blog items accusing me of being racist, and a follow-up complete with this photo of me as a transexual that they doctored up.

They tacked what's supposed to be an Adam's apple. That white stuff they pasted on is supposed to be toilet paper stuffed in my bra. Mmmm, clever! *Original photo by Gregg Sutter.*

It was August when they posted this, there was a presidential election months away, and the country was on the verge of financial collapse, but to these "progressives," what really mattered was answering the question of whether I'm actually a man.

In a month's time, there were almost 3,000 comments on this and other entries attacking me on their site; many or most focusing on this essential issue. Here are a few from their entry, "The 'Lady' Doth Protest Too Much, Methinks," accompanying the photo above:

- Those shoulders belong on a certain NY Giants linebacker from the 1980s. She's a dude, baby.
- For a tranny, she (or he) is not so bad to look at.
- i am pretty sure that amy is actually one of those trany-wannabee women that have adam's apple augmentation surgery.
- The fact is, Amy hasn't had the surgery yet. I found out the hard way, and I'm still shaken up.

- I'd put Amy out of her misery *(kidding! disclaimer! joke! keep your adam's apple square, Amy!)* but apparently U.S military involvement in conflicts abroad is contributing to a worldwide ammunition shortage.

This and their other entries about me were calls to action for their mob of tiny little thugs to turn my comments section into a replica of theirs. A sampling of the hundreds and hundreds of comments they left on my blog:

- Are you a tranny?
- Oh god, I can't resist, I really have to ask: Are you a tranny?
- But seriously . . . you are a tranny, right?

Truth be told, I found their "Amy's a tranny" schtick funny at first, and spent part of an evening annoying my boyfriend by asking him "Can we talk about my penis?" and "Wanna see my package?" Then, I gave the tenor of their attack a little more thought. Here they were, going after me for supposedly being racist by using being trans-gendered and/or transsexual as a put-down. What is this, "Let's fight bigotry with bigotry"?

The goal behind their attacks (beyond their obvious need to kill time) appeared to be punishing me for speech unapproved by "progressives," and intimidating me out of any further "progres-sive" unapproved speech. Their mob took over my comments sec-tion, which exists, in large part, to foster intelligent debate, and did their best to shut down any possibility of it. In fact, those commenting on my site proved themselves shockingly uninterested in learning whether the accusations against me on the "progressive" site actually held any weight. One of the "progressive" bloggers even gloated openly on their blog about the vandalism they were doing to mine:

> I'm starting a betting pool to see which of the subtle vandals and sockpuppets over there she realizes are actually vandalism and not her sack o' shit commenters.

In a matter of hours, dozens of their commenters littered my blog with dozens and dozens of nonsense comments playing on some junior-high in-joke they share. One brave soul used the Tor server (intended to provide Chinese dissidents and the like with a way of secretly surfing and posting on the Net) to defeat my site's spam-blocking defenses. He bragged on their site:

> alright, I'll admit, it was me who got her with Tor— boring Saturday afternoon, what better to do?

Yes, what better to do than leave a steady slew of 30-page pieces of comments spam that had me in tears by Sunday afternoon, as I couldn't scroll down fast enough to the bottom of each to delete it before the next popped up. On the next page is a screenshot of the tail end of one they posted on my entry about their attacks, "This Is Why Our Founding Fathers Fought For Free Speech?"

You suck You suck You suck You suck You suck You
You suck You suck You suck You suck You suck You
You suck You suck You suck You suck You suck You
You suck You suck You suck You suck You suck You
You suck You suck You suck You suck You suck You
You suck You suck You suck You suck You suck You
You suck You suck You suck You suck You suck You
You suck You suck You suck You suck You suck You
You suck You suck You suck You suck You suck You
You suck You suck You suck You suck You suck You
You suck You suck You suck You suck You suck You
You suck You suck You suck You suck You suck You
You suck You suck You suck You suck You suck You
You suck You suck You suck You suck You suck You

Edit | tiny little thugs   Advice
Reply   Goddess
                                      Blog

A tiny section of one of the 30-page pieces of spam they posted on my site.

They began posting comments on my site in my name and the names of my blog regulars—people who are not anonyweenies. Worst of all, these noble crusaders against racism posted a comment with the word "nigger" in the name of the insightful and wryly funny guy who's pretty much my star commenter. Luckily, he stuck around, although I wouldn't have blamed him if he hadn't.

At that point, I started deleting the vandals' comments pretty much wholesale, and banning their IP addresses. Unbelievably, the vandals—like one calling himself "Amy Alkon's Penis"—complained bitterly on their site that I didn't just lie down and let them take over my blog.

The truth is, before their attack, it was almost impossible to get ejected from my blog. Dirty words? Unpopular ideas? Ugly beliefs? Bring 'em on. I'm with Justice Brandeis, who noted "Sunlight is said to be the best of disinfectants."[46] Since I started my blog in May 2003, I'd banned only about four commenters; two of them for masquer-

46 Via Bartleby.com, Louis D. Brandeis, "What Publicity Can Do," *Other People's Money*, chapter 5, p. 92 (1932). First published in *Harper's Weekly*, December 20, 1913.

ading as other real people by posting in those people's names, and the other two for being wildly annoying—but only after my regulars kept begging me to eighty-six 'em. I'm generally known as a staunch supporter of free speech. In fact, I'll defend your right to put up a site attacking my views (perhaps AmyAlkonIsAnAsshat.com if it isn't already taken?) and even your right to pull pictures of me off my site and doctor them up to parody me. If you're clever and funny, I'll probably link to your handiwork. What I won't do is pay for the bandwidth and provide a forum for speech that's intended to quash mine.

Amy Alkon, Private Dick

Most of the tiny little goons from the "progressive" site were careful to drop their little comment turds anonymously. Then, one night, around 2 A.M., a guy got sloppy. I checked my blog comments one last time before going to bed, and found yet another "are you a tranny?"

I unpublished his comment, ran a trace on his IP at ip-adress. com,[47] and got something: an address that traced back to the National Oceanic and Atmospheric Administration (noaa.gov). As I later posted on my blog:

> So . . . get this . . . the commenter is apparently trying to punish me for my free speech...on the government dime. Wait . . . I pay for the government with my tax dollars! On my dime!

---

47 Correctly spelled with one "d."

The guy left his name[48] (in the blacked-out "Commenter" section). It wasn't his full name—it seemed to be his (rather common) last name—but I guessed he might've used it before in commenting on blogs. I Googled it with the name of the "progressive" site, and up popped a commenter there using the same moniker. Next, I Googled his e-mail address, and found it on a comment he'd left on another site—a comment in which he included his first *and* last name. I Googled his full name with noaa.gov, and . . . paydirt!

I went on the NOAA site. At the very top, I noticed the words "Staff Directory." No way. Could it be this easy? I typed in his name, hit "request search," and up he popped: Name, government e-mail address, location, and . . . the best part . . . phone number. I chronicled wha went down from there on my blog:

As long as I had Loserboy's number, hell, why not call it?!

It was the wee hours of the morning, but something told me he was on the job. And, whaddya know, I was right.

His colleague answered the phone and ran to get him. Loserboy got on the line, all gulpy, and pretended he didn't know what I was talking about. I read back his personal e-mail address, and said, so, then, he was telling me somebody was posting from this government IP, using his e-mail address, etc., etc.?

---

48 I've anonymized him, hoping he's learned his lesson.

Not surprisingly, the chickenshit hung up on me.

As you can imagine, *that* dissuaded me!

I called back. Click.

I called back again. He got on the phone and said, in a hard whisper, I couldn't be calling him—he worked for THE GOVERNMENT!

Yeah, no kidding . . . on my dime.

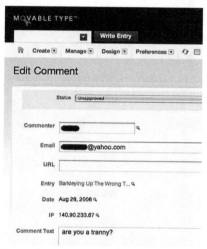

This is the view from within my blog software; only the sections "Commenter" and "Comment Text" would be visible to people visiting my site.

Loserboy P. Smith, whose salary is paid for by you and me while he's posting on my site . . . explained his comment with the following steaming load.

"The pictures I saw from the ('progressive') website made me think I didn't know if you were a male or a female."

I ask him if he seriously thinks I'm transgendered.

"No I don't," he says. "That's why I asked."

Oh, please. Pussyman keeps stonewalling, so I shift my line of questioning, ask him what he does.

Get this, he says he's a satellite controller!

So, I say, "You're supposed to be controlling satellites, but instead you're posting on my site, am I a tranny?"

I say it again, so I can be sure it sinks in: "I'm paying you . . . out of my tax dollars, and you're posting on my site, am I a tranny?"

"I was curious," he says. Right.

"Do you walk up to women in the supermarket and ask them if they're trannies?" I ask him.

He says he doesn't.

"Then why would you do it online?" I ask.

"Because it's different."

"Ohhhh!" I say, "So I'm not really a person. Do you think maybe it would hurt a woman's feelings if you ask her if she's really a man?"

"If I did, I am sorry," he says. "It wasn't my intention."

The Bully Pulpit

If you're throwing a bottle through a store window, you aren't going to tape your business card to it first.

You could say the opportunity for anonymity on the Web brings out the worst in people—or, does it? Are people actually as nasty and uncivilized face-to-face as they come off on the Web, and is the only thing keeping them in check the fear of getting socked in the nose in response? Of course, getting attention is probably a big part of Web nastiness—especially for people who don't get a lot of it in person.

Penny Arcade Web comic artists Jerry Holkins and Mike Krahulik lay the equation out best in "John Gabriel's Greater Internet Fuckwad Theory,"[49] which goes like this:

Normal Person + Anonymity + Audience =
Total Fuckwad

What's worse than one anonymous fuckwad? A whole mob of them. In a mob, a psychological phenomenon called "deindividuation"[50] seems to take hold. A person temporarily loses their individual identity and takes on the identity (and goals) of the mob. As a member of the mob, they're likely to do all sorts of nasty stuff they wouldn't do on their own.

My experience online and off suggests deindividuation happens, and that the anonymity offered by blending into a mass of people is key, but there's a lack of evidence supporting loss of self as the reason for crowd behavior. Social psychologists Tom Postmes and Russell Spears, in an analysis[51] of the body of research on the subject, write that where classic "deindividuation theory argues that the crowd causes a loss of identity, reverting the individual to irrationality," deindividuation might be more accurately redefined as "a shift

---

49 See Penny Arcade's cool green blackboard rendering of it here: http://www.penny-arcade.com/comic/2004/03/19/

50 Coined by social psychologists Leon Festinger, A. Pepitone, and Theodore M. Newcomb in 1952.

51 T. Postmes & R. Spears, "Deindividuation and Anti-Normative Behavior: A Meta-Analysis," *Psychological Bulletin* 123 (1998): 238-259.

from a personal identity to a social identity, shared by the members of a crowd," leading members of that crowd to be more likely to go along with the social norms of the group.

Okay, so if Postmes and Spears are right, the tiny little thugs didn't lose their identity; it shifted. The fact remains: They're mean. As a group. And especially because they're a group of anonyweenies. In the early days of blogs, I sometimes would comment anonymously, but I stopped. It's just too easy to tuck in a low blow. These days, if I'm going to comment on a blog or website, I do it in my own full name. If I won't say something to a person's face, I won't say it about them on the Web.

I do understand that not everybody is as free as I am to slap their name on their opinions, perhaps due to a job or family situation. If, for some reason, you aren't able to post comments in your real name, first and last, can't you at least post *as if you are*? Post as if the person you're remarking on can call you on what you wrote—like I did in this e-mail below to a journalist named Mark Grueter who didn't cover his tracks quite as well as he thought:

Mark,

I saw your comment about me on the entry "Call off the Dogs," on your Hitchens[52] site, pasted in just below—and I have a few questions.

Why is Hitch hitting on that dog?[53]
Mark G | 10.02.08 - 4:01 am | #

---

52 Christopher Hitchens.

53 The blog item he posted his little nasty on included a photograph of me talking to Hitchens.

Do you think I'm a "dog"?

Do you normally go around to women announcing to them what you think of their looks?

Would you say that to me if you were standing across from me in public?

Do you think that, perhaps because you disagree with some of my thinking, it's appropriate to post that about me?

Do you even know what my thinking is, or are you just following the crowd, and I'm the designated kickball?

Do you consider this "progressive" behavior?

Do you think the others on your site are more careful to hide their identities because they can attack people without accountability?

I'm giving you the opportunity to answer because I'm putting this in my book. I want to know how a guy like you ends up behaving like such a boor on the Internet.

—Amy Alkon

Surprise, surprise. Grueter never wrote back.

10

IT'S NICE TO BE NICE

We can look at strangers we encounter in one of two ways—as people or as sweating, farting, masses of flesh we wish would get the hell out of our way. Unfortunately, the latter view is what comes naturally to us, so a weekend afternoon trying to park and shop at a new supermarket near my house can feel like stepping onto the streets of Fallujah—in a red, white, and blue "Support Our Troops!" teddy.

Remember, although we're living in vast, modern societies, we're guided by quaint Stone Age brains, perfect for life within a small tribe where everybody knows everybody. Since we lack the natural social policing of a small, contained society, we're free to flip each other the bird, force loud cell phone conversations on the rest of the checkout line, and tuck a softball of snotted-up Kleenex into the airline seat pocket for the next passenger.

Going after the flagrantly rude isn't enough. Because we're hardwired to be nice to people we know—while living mostly among people we don't—we need to go out of our way to treat all these nobodies like somebodies. Obviously, if lots of us start nice-ing it up regularly, the overall niceness level of society will go up a notch. Of course, some people will still act like jerks and hop a free ride on the efforts of the rest of us. Those people aren't so clever. It turns out that the bumper sticker that pretty much comes standard on every aging Volvo, "Perform random acts of kindness . . ." isn't just hippie-dippy hoohah. It's actually in the self-interest of each of us to go out of our way for other people; even total strangers.

Many people recognize this intuitively. The title of this chapter, "It's Nice To Be Nice," was the motto of Henry's restaurant in Algonac, Michigan, and it echoes numerous bits of popular wisdom, including Malcolm Forbes' prescription, "The more sympathy you give, the less you need" and the Dalai Lama's advice, "If you want to be happy, practice compassion." But, these really are more than warm fuzzies to needlepoint onto couch pillows or fodder for the inoffensive office decor industry. There's now data showing that you're likely to be happier if you help others.

Don't be yourself, be someone a little nicer.
—Mignon McLauglin, *The Second Neurotic's Notebook,* 1966

"Positive psychology" professor Sonja Lyubomirsky takes an evidence-based approach to happiness. She and her team at UC Riverside have conducted a number of studies that strongly suggest helping others really does bring happiness, and that performing acts of kindness on a regular basis makes people happy for an extended period.

In one of Lyubomirsky's experiments, participants were asked to perform five kind acts a week for six weeks. The acts could be large or small—even just thanking someone for their hard work. The researchers not only found that being kind and generous made people happy, but that those who did their entire week's generosity assignment on a single day experienced a significant elevation in their happiness—suggesting that it's really, really nice to be really, really nice.

The researchers also found that those who were required to perform the same three acts of kindness every week for 10 weeks had their level of happiness drop in the middle of the study. (It eventually rebounded to their original level.) Lyubomirsky speculates in her book *The How of Happiness* that the repetition turned their exercise into just another chore. She feels that acts of kindness must remain fresh and meaningful to enhance well-being, which, to me, says they have to come from the heart, from genuine concern for others and their needs. You can't just make a list, "1. Help three little old ladies cross street," then start forcing them across at gunpoint so you can get on with your day.

To explain why being good to others makes you happier, Lyubomirsky cites evidence from past psychological research. Doing kind deeds can, for example, distract you from your problems, encourage you to be grateful for how good you have it (gratitude being another major happiness producer), and can lead to a more positive self-image and a greater sense of meaning in your own life.[54] She adds that "kind-

---

54 M.C. Clark (ed.), *Prosocial Behavior: Review of Personality and Social Psychology* (vol. 12, pp. 238-64). Newbury Park, CA: Sage.

ness can jump-start a cascade of positive social consequences," leading people to like you, appreciate you, offer you gratitude and even friendship, and maybe reciprocate in *your* times of need.[55]

Lyubomirsky illustrates the benefits of reaching out to others with the story of five women with multiple sclerosis who became peer supporters for 67 other MS patients.[56] The five women were trained in "active and compassionate listening" and told to call each patient for 15 minutes once a month. In interviews, these peer supporters told the researchers that they'd experienced dramatic changes in their lives as a result of their volunteer work. They were less focused on their own problems, and felt increased satisfaction and feelings of mastery. They gained a stronger sense of self-esteem and self-acceptance, and developed confidence in their ability to cope with difficulties and manage their disease. As one woman said, "There's no cure for MS, but I really feel that I'm able to handle whatever comes my way."

Amazingly, the positive changes in the lives of the five peer supporters far outpaced the benefits for those they were supporting. Most notably, the volunteers experienced a boost in their general life satisfaction seven times greater than that shown by the patients they helped. Also, the benefits the volunteers experienced from their kind acts grew as time went on—"an incredible finding," Lyubomirsky

---

55 R. Trivers, "The Evolution of Reciprocal Altruism," *Quarterly Review of Biology,* 46 (1971): 35-57.

56 A three-year study by C.E. Schwartz and M. Sendor, "Helping Others Helps Oneself: Response Shift Effects in Peer Support, *Social Science and Medicine,* 48 (1999): 1563-75.

writes, given that the benefits seen in most happiness experiments "tend to diminish over time."

I experience a similarly remarkable high from a program I started in 2007 to demystify "making it" for "at-risk" kids. Once a month, I go to a Los Angeles high school and talk for a couple hours to try to give the students a sense of what's possible, even for kids who don't come from privilege, if they're willing to work hard. I don't have federal funding—or any funding. It's not even a formal program, just me and a teacher who doesn't seem to mind me bugging her to schedule me in to speak to classes.

I talk about my work, but I also tell them stuff I wish somebody would've told me in high school, and give them real-world examples to help them see that you "don't have to 'be' your circumstances." I can tell, right as I'm talking, that a lot of the kids are getting something out of it, and that's so incredibly elevating, it's like they're doing me a favor by letting me try to help them. The truth is, I'd pay to feel the way I do when I walk out of that school.

Christmas Comes But 365 Days a Year

No, I don't believe a fat guy in a red suit will pull up next to your chimney and drop a Sony PlayStation down the flue if you served soup at the homeless shelter this year. But, in principle, that isn't off-base—nor is the Siddhartha-as-Santa idea of karma. Karma, as it's understood by the average person, is the comforting but evidence-free belief that people will get what they deserve because there's some cosmic accountant keeping score. (Yeah, go ahead and be a bitch—just don't come crying to me when you come back as a dung beetle.)

In reality, it seems there's a hardwired behavioral scorekeeping module in each of us, helping us suss out who's naughty and nice. Research by evolutionary psychologists and economists has shown that those who give nice get nice in return.[57] The official term for this is "reciprocal altruism," but unofficially, it's called "tit-for-tat" or "don't be a greedy bastard or you'll get yours." The give nice/get nice strategy is optimal for deciding how to treat people in a group where everybody knows everybody and reputation is a factor, but in a one-time interaction with a stranger, there's no possibility for reciprocity or punishment in the absence of it. Yet, most people don't go around stiffing highway truck stop waitresses out of a tip or doing other skeevy things to people they aren't likely to run into again.

Research by Cornell economist Robert H. Frank and others suggests that, by doing good for another person, even someone you know you'll never see again, you're doing good for yourself. This isn't just because it feels good to be good, and bad to be a conniving creep.[58] By being a generous person, you're probably putting out a psychic press release about yourself, signaling to others that you're the kind

---

57 K. Clark and M.Sefton, "The Sequential Prisoner's Dilemma: Evidence on Reciprocation." *Economic Journal* 111, 51-68. (Just one example of many.)

58 Eighteenth-century economist Adam Smith (briefly referenced in Chapter 9) speculated that "moral sentiments"—emotions like pity and compassion and a feeling of fellowship with other men—compel man to extend himself for others, and to "render their happiness necessary to him, though he derives nothing from it, except the pleasure of seeing it." Frank builds on Smith's work, writing in *Passions Within Reason* that if a person "is emotionally predisposed to regard cheating as an unpleasurable act in and of itself—that is, if he has a conscience—he will be better able to resist the temptation to cheat."

of person who deserves their generosity. In *Passions Within Reason*, Frank, referencing the work of psychologist Paul Ekman, describes how people telegraph the way they're likely to behave with their facial muscle and eye movement, body language, vocal expression, and "microexpressions"—facial expressions present for a fleeting moment that convey how a person really feels.

Remarkably, even strangers seem able to discern which people are givers and which are not—with surprising accuracy. Frank details an experiment he and his colleagues[59] ran in which participants talked to strangers for 30 minutes, and were then asked to guess how they'd behave in a subsequent game. The participants' predictions of which people would be self-serving hogs were correct a whopping 56.8 percent of the time—more than twice the pure chance accuracy rate of 26.3 percent.

This study, like many others, suggests that your reputation really does precede you—even when you encounter a person you've never met before who's never heard word one about you. Just smile, and you might tell them everything they need to know about you; which, let's hope, won't be "better bolt down anything of value when she's around."

Good Is Catching

Contrary to a decades-long propaganda campaign by mothers and kindergarten teachers, you probably can "make" somebody do something, probably by doing it first. We're a monkey-see/monkey-do species, and social norms get set one person at a time. That nice begets

---

59 Tom Gilovich and Dennis Regan.

nice and nasty begets nasty is common sense to most people, but it's also borne out by research like the famous 1968 "lost" wallet studies by psychologist Harvey Hornstein and his colleagues.[60] In one version of their study, they kept leaving what appeared to be a lost wallet inside an unsealed envelope on a New York City sidewalk. The envelope was addressed to the owner of the wallet, and also contained a letter, apparently written by the person who'd found the wallet to the person who'd lost it. There were three versions of the letter: positive, negative, and neutral. The neutral version was matter-of-fact:

> Dear Mr. Erwin: I found your wallet which I am returning. Everything is here just as I found it.

The positive and negative letters included the sender's feelings about returning the wallet. The positive one said:

> I must say that it has been a pleasure to be able to help somebody in the small things that make life nicer. It's really been no problem at all and I'm glad to help.

The negative version included this little rant:

> I must say that taking responsibility for the wallet and having to return it has been a great inconvenience. I was quite

---

60 H. A. Hornstein, E. Fisch, and M. Holmes, "Influence of a Model's Feelings about His Behavior and His Relevance as a Comparison of Other Observers' Helping Behavior," *Journal of Personal and Social Psychology*, 10 (1968): 222-26.

annoyed at having to bother with the whole problem of
returning it. I hope you appreciate the efforts that I have
gone through.

Sixty percent of the wallets with positive letters were returned,
and 51 percent of those with neutral letters, but only 18 percent of
those with negative letters; chances were, because even the tiniest
social norms—like the tone set by a single person—establish a standard for behavior for those who follow.

Because the status quo—the way things are—is a social norm
itself, changing it takes applying entrepreneurial thinking to day-to-
day life. While many people will only question or stand up against
behavior they see as egregiously wrong, entrepreneurial thinkers are
constantly taking a critical look at the world around them, figuring
out how it could be improved, and speaking up or taking action.
This is second nature to some, but anybody can train him- or herself to think this way, just by getting in the habit of asking "What's
wrong with this picture?" or "What could be more right about this
picture, and what would it take to get it that way?" Sometimes, all it
takes is one person to shine a light on a problem for a lot of people
to pitch in.

That's what happened after I heard a businessman, well-dressed,
late 50s, with a reptilian air, chatting up a guy I often saw doing
intricate ink and marker drawings at a Santa Monica Starbucks. The
artist had the look of homelessness—leathered skin and the hollow
cheeks of somebody who's a stranger to regular meals—but his hair
was pulled back into a neat ponytail and his plaid shirt buttoned all
the way to the top, like he was doing his best to keep up appearances.

I'd always admired him, both for the beauty of his drawings, and for how tirelessly he worked on them, day and night, always at the back table at that Starbucks.

"Do you sell your work?" the businessman asked the artist. From the grimace on the artist's face, I guessed he was thinking "Not to you," but he nodded and muttered yes. The artist waited for the guy to make an offer. None came. He shifted uncomfortably, rearranging his pens. Finally, the businessman spoke: "How much do you want for it?" Clever. He must've read a few of those wheeler-dealer books that come in so handy when negotiating with the talented homeless. I could see the artist doing the math in his head: Be true to himself or possibly get a sandwich. He hung his head, offering tentatively, "Ten dollars?"

Now, even if the guy's work isn't your style, I think you can appreciate that his drawings are beautiful, intricate, and worth more than 10 bucks. Surely, the buyer would do the right thing, and toss in some extra cash. Wrong. He peeled off $20 for two drawings, and handed it to the artist. After he picked the two out, he ordered the artist to sign them. The artist stood and picked up a pen. "Wait!" the guy said. "Let me see your signature first!" The artist made a motion to accommodate him, but the businessman stopped him, saying he'd changed his mind; he'd just take the drawings signature-free. Yeah, erase all traces of the homeless guy, stick the thing in a $700 frame, and your friends will think you bought it at a gallery for $7,000.

Even ickier, the discount-squeezing art patron apparently felt entitled to a little bonding time with the creator of his purchases. He started going on and on about what great art the guy was making. I couldn't keep my mouth shut a moment longer. "If you do think it's

"Zuma," by Gary Musselman

"Power," by Gary Musselman

"Progress," by Gary Musselman

such great art—and it is; they're beautiful—shouldn't you be paying more than $10 apiece?" The creep retorted that he would have paid up to $15, but no more. I glared at him and said, "Because you can get away with paying a very low price for something doesn't mean you should." I told him I wasn't in a position to buy art (at least, not at what I felt was a fair price), but I thought they were beautiful, and worth at least $100. The artist came over and took my hand in his, looked into my eyes and whispered thank you. I complimented him again on his work, and said people shouldn't be paying bargain prices for it.

The next day, I was having breakfast at the Rose Café when the businessman spotted me. Leaning across my table, he snarled, "You made that artist feel SMALL!" ("That artist?" After talking to the guy and practically stealing his work did he not even know the guy's name?) He hissed that he and the artist had a "wonderful moment" going after he'd bought the art, and I'd ruined it by butting in. "On the contrary," I said, "It was ugly. You gouged a homeless guy. He was grateful I spoke up."

After the businessman left, I got to wondering, is it possible I had made the artist feel bad? I went back to Starbucks to look for him. He smiled broadly when he saw me. "God bless you for what you did," he said. "You're the first woman in my life who hasn't taken advantage of me."

His name is Gary Musselman, and he did happen to be homeless. It turns out he didn't want to sell his drawings to the guy; in fact, he *hated* selling them to the guy. He also knew they were worth much more than $10, but he was hungry. "It's not fair; it's real cruel. But that's the way it is," he said.

I posted a blog item telling the story above, illustrated with photos of Gary's drawings, at around noon on a Sunday. By noon on Monday there were $1,500 in offers to buy his art and an offer to provide him with free legal service. My friend Jackie Danicki built him a blog to showcase his work. People bought his drawings because they loved them—that was clear from the comments they left on my site. But, when I told them they couldn't pay by PayPal or check, they drove long distances to give him cash. One of the baristas at Starbucks let faraway buyers pay into his PayPal account, then gave Gary the money. From down the block and around the world, there was an amazing outpouring of generosity of spirit from people building on the outpouring they saw from other people. I just started it by being a meddling busybody, then publishing the blog item.

One of my regular blog commenters, Canadian software designer Robert Werner, set off a similar chain reaction in 2005 after a friend of his bought a new computer just before Christmas. She asked him what she could do with the "perfectly good" one, only a few years old, that she was replacing. Werner thought about it, and advertised it on Craigslist, offering it free to a charitable organization, somebody who couldn't afford a computer, or to needy kids.

Within 24 hours, nearly 50 people responded. Of these, he felt nine were truly in need—which left him with a problem. He couldn't leave the other eight in the lurch. On his blog, Pelausa.blogspot.com, he published a call for people to donate their old computers, and got five. A few weeks later, the *Vancouver Courier* and BCTV did stories on his project, and within a few days, 800 offers had poured in, and people were dropping off computers at his apartment round the clock. Werner and his friends, neighbors, and colleagues worked like crazy to refurbish them, his mom stuck a big red ribbon around each one, and he and a friend spent Christmas driving around delivering them.

One of these computers went to Tanya and Radu Sitar, Romanian emigrants who'd arrived in Vancouver just two months before with their two young twins and little beyond the clothes on their backs. Their computer allowed them to apply for jobs online and stay in touch with their families in Romania, and helped them get to know their new country and culture. After getting the computer, Tanya told a TV news reporter about Werner and his team, "I can't . . . I can't . . . thank them . . . probably I will never find a way to thank them, but I know there is a god."

Werner realized there were many people lacking the means to buy a computer, and many people and companies with computer equipment to donate; they just needed to be connected. He turned his little Christmas project into the all-volunteer BC Digital Divide (BCDigitalDivide.org), taking in three-to-five-year-old computers, refurbishing them, and giving them out to needy families.[61] Werner, who had a full-time software consulting business and a new company in the works, couldn't maintain the level of involvement he had over the holidays, so he put the word out for volunteers. Up popped Bruce

---

61 Werner had been commenting on my blog for probably a year before I found out about his program, and only because I asked for stories where one person's act of generosity or kindness inspired other people to follow suit. When I e-mailed him that I was impressed that he'd never mentioned it until I made the request, he wrote back, "People who endlessly talk about their accomplishments just reveal to me a deep insecurity. I don't always succeed but I always try to do rather than talk about doing."

Steven, the Mr. Fix-It of the Vancouver School Board, and Bob Rogers, a 70-something retired BC Tel employee. These two now do the bulk of the work, but countless others, including Werner, pitch in as well.

Werner marvels at the difference the donated computers have made in people's lives. Tanya Sitar used the computer her family got to land a job as a teacher's aide. A few months later, the Sitars were able to afford a new computer of their own so they gave the donated computer to a newly arrived family from Romania. Werner was thrilled. "As you can see, one small act of kindness inspires another, which inspires another, and so on. Too many people wait for others or the government to reach out that first time, when they themselves fully have it within their power to do a lot on their own."

You don't have to start or join an organization to make a difference. My sister Caroline, who lives in San Francisco, wanted to do something to help people in need, so she called some volunteer organizations. And called. And called. No one called her back. When she finally got someone on the phone, she learned there were all these requirements and some long orientation (to be trained to do something she already does professionally). She gave up on the idea of joining somebody else's effort, and thought about what people need and what she could do on her own.

She walks a few miles a day for exercise, and likes to putter around in the kitchen, so every week, she makes sandwiches by the loaf and tromps around San Francisco handing them out to hungry people. On her walks, she sees a guy who's a Vietnam vet. "He was in one of those tiny little planes, doing the bombing," she says. He tells her things about his mom and his life. "He's been around the world.

He had a sailboat for a while. And he's just kind of interesting." Now, she brings him a sandwich a couple times a week, and they talk.

She told me there are places where volunteers assemble lunches or dinners and put them in boxes, but that wasn't for her. "I like the direct contact. I really like people, and I like knowing about people and where they're from and what their story is."

But, say you don't have the time or inclination to start some program of your own. You don't have to do anything big or organized. We're all large, easily wounded children. Showing concern for a stranger, even in the smallest way, makes a difference. You're telling them they matter—and, by doing that, you'll probably get the message back that you matter, too. It seems so stunningly obvious: In a world in which so many people feel increasingly alienated, if you want to stop feeling alienated, just act connected.

Because extending yourself for strangers doesn't come naturally, you'll have to make an effort to pay attention to them and consider how the things you do or don't do will affect them. As for what you shouldn't do, it pretty much boils down to "don't inflict yourself on other people." Don't be a distracted driver—you might hurt somebody or make them late for work. Don't take two parking spaces because you're too lazy to re-park in just one. Don't leave your coffee cup and a table full of scone crumbs for the next person. Clean up after your dog—even when you're pretty sure nobody's looking. Flush.

Regarding what you should do, if you just train yourself to extend your concern to others, it'll come to you. Sonja Lyubomirsky, one of the least sappy people ever to make a career out of happiness, echoes that thought: "I have come across numerous books, magazine articles, and Web sites advocating doing acts of kindness, and I always get the sense, perhaps unfounded, that they patronize the reader a bit. If you decide to become a more generous, compassionate, and giving person, you will know what you should do."

It really is the simplest stuff. Lyubomirsky gives a few examples—babysitting for a harried parent when you weren't asked, traveling to see a friend in need, putting money in somebody's meter, and "smiling at somebody who needed a smile even when it was the hardest thing to do at that very moment." Or, maybe, like me, you're in the habit of going to a coffeehouse and reading the newspaper over breakfast. After you're done with it, look around. See somebody who just walked in who's scanning the place for something; maybe a paper? Get their attention and ask if they'd like yours. Totally minor gesture, minuscule expenditure of thought and energy. Yet, more often than not, it bowls people over: the fact that a stranger noticed them, thought about their needs, and went out of her way for them, totally unasked. And, if you really want to amaze somebody right out of their socks, look for a person eating alone without anything to read, bring your paper over, and ask them if they'd like it. I'm not exaggerating when I say I've seen on people's faces a flash of something that reads like there just might be hope for humanity.

ACKNOWLEDGMENTS

This book is in memory of my friend Cathy Seipp, who died of cancer at 49. Cathy was as irate at injustice, bad manners, and wanton stupidity as I am, and a cracklingly smart and funny writer (check out her piece on Naomi Wolf in *reason* magazine).

When I was going back and forth between New York and L.A., I read Cathy's *New York Press* column, "Letter From Los Angeles," and wrote her a fan letter. She read my *New York Daily News* column, brought me into her circle, and we started our monthly "writergirl breakfast" at the Farmers Market. The regulars were all Cathy's smart and talented writer friends—who quickly became my friends: Nancy Rommelmann, Hillary Johnson, Emmanuelle Richard, Sandra Tsing Loh, Kate Coe, Samantha Dunn, Jill Stewart, Denise Hamilton, Kerry Madden Lunsford, Meredith Brody, and Irene Lacher. In short order, you all made me feel L.A. was home.

My editorial assistant Stephanie Willen read every word in this book about 26 times, challenged me on anything and everything questionable, and had the integrity to keep at me until I listened.

She's a wonderful editor, talented writer, and compelling thinker who will soon be publishing books of her own.

My man Gregg Sutter is the best person I know—that rare guy you can count on to do the right thing when nobody's looking. He read and commented on every chapter and shot the beautiful photo of me on the cover. While I'm not allowed to prank anyone when I'm with him, I know I can always, always count on him for bail.

My editor John Aherne, at McGraw-Hill, is a truly good human being and a wise and talented editor who made this a better book . . . and gave me a really long leash!

I was terrified about the copyediting process, which I imagined as a sort of literary Sherman's March to the Sea, but I got really lucky with McGraw-Hill's Nancy Hall. She's a writer's copyeditor who worked to understand the quirks of my writing style, and only corrected my unintentional errors.

Thanks to everybody at McGraw-Hill for the way you've all been behind me and this book, which really means a lot. Thanks especially to Heather Cooper in marketing; Tom Lau, who designed the cover; and Ann Pryor in publicity.

I'm grateful to have Betsy Amster as my agent. She's wise, patient, and kind; has great taste and literary judgment; is there for me when the chips are down; and sticks to her guns when she thinks I'm making a mistake.

Many, many thanks to the members of HBES, the Human Behavior And Evolution Society, and NEEPS, the Northeast Evolutionary Psychology Society for being extraordinarily generous and welcoming to me from day one. Thanks especially to David Buss, Jerome Barkow, David Sloan Wilson, Steve Gaulin, A.J. Figueredo,

Lisa Zunshine, Alan Kugel, Satoshi Kanazawa, and finally, to Peter J. Richerson who went out of his way to direct me to the research that became the foundation of this book.

Thanks to my posse of blog commenters, Crid, Radwaste, Eric, Marion, Deidre, Pirate Jo, Purple Pen, Brian, Martin, Robert W, Norman, Patrick, Momof4, lujlp, lovelysoul, Conan The Grammarian, Gog_Magog_Carpet_Reclaimers, and all the rest. Like Cathy Seipp, I swore I'd never write for free, but you make it worth my while.

Thank you to everybody from the 18th Street Coffee House, especially Linda, Samantha, Angus, Keith, Mariano, Ella, Adrian, Erin, Miguel, and Jesse. Here's to the world's cutest senior citizen lovebirds—Kay, who lights up the place, and Earl, who lights up Kay—and to all the regulars slaving away on their books, screenplays, lesson plans, and dissertations. P.S. I'm leaving in five minutes and you can have my table next to the plug.

Thanks to Sander Greenland for his fierceness in battling the purveyors of shoddy and deceptive data, for helping me recognize them, and for teaching me about satisficing, which enabled me to finish this book well before turning 90.

Here's to all the editors who run my Advice Goddess column, and especially, to everybody in the alt weekly world. Thanks to everybody who reads my syndicated advice column in their local newspaper. If you aren't reading me, please write and ask them to run my column!

A number of people in my life have been especially supportive. David Wallis has been a great friend in so many ways since I met him at NYU's housing office in 1986 on my third day in New York. Emily Tarr "adopted" me when I got to New York, introduced me to Paris, and has been a great friend on both continents. Merci to Emily and the rest of my Paris posse—Mark Gaito, Chantal Janisson, and Pierre—who make Paris even more than it already is. My friend Susan Shapiro is an extraordinarily generous human being and a talented writer and writing teacher who knows more about how to sell books and articles than probably anybody else on the planet. Thanks for FKW, too, Sue. Like Sue, biographer David Rensin, my "literary conscience," bugged me to write a book for years, and Jackie Danicki annoyed me until I agreed to write this particular book. Bruce David at *Hustler* couldn't believe the *L.A. Times Magazine* turned down my telemarketers story and he snapped it up. Glenn Sacks and some of the guys in the men's movement have rallied behind me when I've been under attack. Caroline Belli, my little sister, is as good-hearted as she is wise. My friend Andrew Siegel was there for me from the start, and Allison McDonell, Lydia Prior, and Xenia Shin were there for me in the middle, editing my column and reading parts of this book. Deborah Levin is a wonderful, loving friend who never ceases to amaze me with her warmth and the way she sees the world. Kaja Perina and Nando Pelusi have been very supportive. Marlon Brando was a good friend who believed in me as a writer before anybody did. Goldstar.com's Jim McDonald is smarter about business than anybody I know, and was never too busy building a multi-city company to get on the phone and strategize about my cover or other issues. Kelly Boston, a talented writer, really great mother, and good friend, read much of this book, gave me wise advice, and fed me when my fridge was bare. Sophie, Oliver, Avery, Victor, and Cheryl Houser made me part of their New York family. On the left coast, Kelly Boston, Lee Olvera, Jude, and Lilly have done the same. And then there's Sergeant

Heather, Heather Rudomin, a wonderful friend, brilliant mother, and one of the smartest women I know, who's always giving me another reason to be in awe of her.

There are the friends besides Cathy who I've lost: Marlowe Minnick, whose humor and sensibility remain a huge influence on mine, and Marnye Oppenheim, whose fierceness, funny writing, and friendship I miss very much.

This book wouldn't have been possible without *San Jose Metro*'s editor and publisher, Dan Pulcrano, who built me a website against my will in 1998.

And, finally, thank you to librarians everywhere, and especially to the Farmington Hills, Michigan, librarians from 1970 to 1982.